Images of Eternity

Images of Eternity

L. D. JOHNSON

MARION JOHNSON
COMPILER

BROADMAN PRESS
Nashville, Tennessee

© Copyright 1984 • Broadman Press
All rights reserved.
4253-42
ISBN: 0-8054-5342-3

Quotations marked GNB are from the *Good News Bible,* the Bible in Today's English Version. Old Testament: Copyright © American Bible Society, 1976; New Testament: Copyright © American Bible Society 1966, 1971, 1976. Used by permission.

Quotations marked *The Jerusalem Bible* are from *The Jerusalem Bible,* © 1966 by Darton, Longman and Todd, Ltd. and Doubleday and Company, Inc. Used by permission of the publisher.

Quotations marked Moffatt are from *The Bible: a New Translation* by James A. R. Moffatt. Copyright © 1935 by Harper and Row, Publishers, Inc. Used by permission.

Quotations marked NEB are from *The New English Bible.* Copyright © The Delegates of the Oxford University Press and The Syndics of the Cambridge University Press, 1961, 1970. Reprinted by permission.

Quotations marked KJV are from the King James Version of the Bible.

All other Scripture quotations not credited within the text are from the Revised Standard Version of the Bible, copyrighted 1946, 1952, © 1971, 1973.

Dewey Decimal Classification: 248.4
Subject Heading: CHRISTIAN LIFE
Library of Congress Catalog Card Number: 84-4987
Printed in the United States of America

Library of Congress Cataloging in Publication Data

Johnson, L. D., 1916-1981
  Images of eternity.

  Sequel to: Moments of reflection.
  1. Meditations.   I. Johnson, Marion E., 1914-
II. Johnson, L. D., 1916-1981. Moments of reflection.
III. Title.
BV4832.2.J613   1984   242   84-4987
ISBN 0-8054-5342-3

To
Rebecca Johnson
who was born
too late to remember
her grandfather

A Tribute

L. D. Johnson was a giant.
His mind was sharp as a Damascus blade.
His heart encompassed the whole human family.
His spirit soared with the freedom of "just men made perfect."
His vision pierced our provincialism, our prejudice, and our pride.
His patience endured hardness with the faith and fortitude of Job.
His compassion reached out to everybody who was hurting or about to hurt.
His friendship flamed brightly to warm the lives of multitudes.
His courage was undaunted by principalities or powers.
His whole life and ministry were everlastingly laid on the line for truth and justice and reconciliation and mercy and peace.

L. D. Johnson's great gifts are still blessing us, his smile is still encouraging us, his strength is still supporting us, his wisdom is still instructing us, his biblical faith is still lifting us, his churchmanship is still inspiring us, and his words such as these in this book are still speaking to us.

                                  Foy Valentine
                                  Executive Director
                                  The Christian Life Commission
                                  of the Southern Baptist Convention

Contents

Foreword
Preface
I.
Had I Not Seen the Sun 13
II.
A Future and a Hope 23
III.
Making the Living Worthwhile 33
IV.
What Is There to Be Grateful About? 40
V.
O Come, Emmanuel 50
VI.
Don't Wait for Agreement 62
VII.
Baffling Reflections in a Mirror 75
VIII.
Life's Unexpected Dividends 85
IX.
What Is the Bible to Us? 95
X.
Coping with the Shadow 107
XI.
Time to Spare for God 117

Foreword

We are living in a time of "no faith" and "easy faith." So many of the people who attract media attention, for example, have either dismissed faith altogether or are espousing some self-serving and simplistic expression of faith. On the same television set you can hear God both scorned and credited with winning a basketball championship.

I am not helped by either extreme. I am helped by people for whom faith is real, realistic, and a creative struggle. I have been helped a lot by L. D. Johnson.

Great faith is never easy faith. Great faith invariably has been through the furnaces of suffering or doubt or some other hardship. It has distressed places and scorch marks on it.

Precisely in this sense, L. D. Johnson was a person of great faith. It showed physically. He looked like someone who had survived an impossible journey, but whom the ordeal had left exceptionally wise. And that is what he was.

Wisdom. Rarest of gifts. Not to be confused with mere intelligence. Isaiah asked, "Where then are your wise men?" (18:12). James inquired, "Who is wise and understanding among you?" and answered, "By his good life let him show his works in the meekness of wisdom" (3:13). L. D. was wise, by the Bible's definition.

One suspects that the Bible today is being much more recommended than read. Many praise and defend it who scarcely know it. L. D. knew the inner world of the Bible like the city in which he lived. His uncommon familiarity with this world made him an extraordinary guide, and he was never more effective than when he was interpreting its meaning for contemporary living. He was genuinely biblical, both at the level of technical scholarship and in the depths of his heart.

During the Greenville years, while he was pastor of First Baptist Church and chaplain at Furman University, L. D. became something of a prophet and priest to the entire community. Through a weekly newspaper column, he inspired, challenged, and instructed thousands of readers. His gracious wife, Marion, has done all of us a service by compiling this collection of some of those columns.

Jeremiah wrote of the day when the life of the people of God would be "like a watered garden" (31:12). Those of us who were privileged to share a part of the journey with L. D. found so much of God's intention for all of us fulfilled in him. His life, "like a watered garden," was a source of faith, hope, and love for many, many people. We will miss him all the days of our lives, and will turn often to his words for wisdom and for blessed memories.

C. DAVID MATTHEWS
Pastor, First Baptist Church
Greenville, South Carolina

Preface

L. D. Johnson's ministry took on many forms. He was perhaps most exposed to the general public through a series of editorials which he wrote for various newspapers in the Southeast. The writing of these articles spanned at least two decades. It was another way that he could share his wisdom, humor, goodness, and faith.

One of my father's favorite illustrations concerning making life fully meaningful comes from the Bible. King Hezekiah was so elated at learning that God had promised him fifteen more years of life despite a serious illness he foolishly received the envoys of Babylon who said they had only come to wish him well. Isaiah, realizing that they had really come to look at the defenses of Judah, informed the king that Babylon would be back to destroy their land. Hezekiah responded, "Why not, if there will be peace and security in *my* days?"

That line always intrigued my father. He saw it as a totally self-centered, short-sighted stance in life. He saw that cavalier attitude as unacceptable. I remember one of the things he said about one of the past presidents of Furman University. Speaking of this man's vision of greatness for the University, he said, "Blessed is the man who plants trees, the shade of which he knows he will never sit under."

For many decades and in several different environments, my father was a nurturer of people. Nurturing is not always an easy or satisfying task. Sometimes he needed to shake the old foliage off. Often the root systems needed feeding. The soil around the roots needed reworking. He could lead people to the deep springs of living water. Often as painful as it was for him who nurtured, pruning was necessary for those who were misshapened and twisted. When there was new, tender growth, he did what he could to protect it, but his goal always was to help individuals grow strong enough to stand alone in any kind of environmental condition. It was weary, back-breaking work. Often those who benefited did not or could not fathom the all-consuming effort he would make for someone who was about to wither and die, or whose growth had been stunted.

Six and a half years before his death, he learned about the illness that would take his life. He had already faced so much personal grief and pain. He had already received so much personal and professional satisfaction and fulfillment, why not use this new knowledge as the occasion to terminate the long hours, the striving, the giving that always comes with nurturing? He could not look at all he had done and all he was to those of us who loved him and simply tip his hat, asking, "Why not, if there can be peace in my day?"

But despite the pain and discomfort of surgery and radiation, despite the strength-sapping effects of chemotherapy, despite unimaginable inconveniences, he continued to make the same trek to the field, using the same tools of love, compassion, patience, confrontation, and integrity. He went on giving and nurturing. Many who have tried to be objective have stated that the last six and a half years of his ministry were the most effective. Those years constituted the jewel in his crown. Truly then he nurtured, knowing full well he would never enjoy the shade or see the fruits of the ones for whom he tended.

The newspaper articles included in this book are from that period of his ministry. They are among the very best that he wrote. They were collected and edited with the hope that even after his death the nurturing process can be enhanced. They are shared with the faith and assurance that in the days to come others who never knew the man may glean nourishment and support from his gifts. It is the hope of both my mother and myself that this volume will be received in the spirit of the one in whose memory it is given. His spirit refused simply to accept peace and ease for himself in his own time, but always toiled as a gardener in the service of the One whose creations we all are.

C. ROLAND JOHNSON
Pastor, First Baptist Church
Jefferson, Georgia

I
Had I Not Seen the Sun

1

Easter's special meaning arises from our common experiences with death, and the life-renewing experiences of resurrection. We die, not just once, but daily. Death of the physical body is the final and most awesome death-event, but dying takes many forms. Faith dies; hope perishes; love is extinguished.

But can there be a resurrection? Dare one hope for newness? Is liberation from the bondage of sin and self-destructiveness a lively possibility? Can people who have buried their promises to each other in a grave of mutual disillusionment and distrust hope for a resurrection?

Easter says: Yes, yes, yes. Never despair. Do not surrender hope. Don't give up. Resist believing that death is the final enactment. See, there is life beyond the death of life. The grave continually is forced to give up her prize.

When you experience resurrection, you cannot go on living routinely, much less hopelessly. Shedding one's graveclothes is no "What's new?" event. You are not the same after resurrection.

Emily Dickinson, Amherst's little wren of a maiden perpetually dressed as a bride, knew about the vision of new life: "Had I not seen the sun I could have borne the shade; but light a newer wilderness my wilderness has made." To see the sun is to be made forever dissatisfied with living in the shade.

Do you know anyone who has experienced resurrection? Have you yourself seen the sun? If so, you know that the shade will no longer do. You must live in the sunlight, because that is where you have found life.

In a most readable book written about the Bible, Robert McAfee Brown records the story of just such an experience. A group of Marines returning to the States from serving in Japan after World War II approached a chaplain on board the transport ship with them and asked him to lead them in a Bible study class each morning.

Swallowing his amazement, the chaplain jumped at the chance. One day near the end of the trip they were studying John 11, the account of Jesus raising Lazarus from the dead. The chaplain explained that the miracle was not simply about the reanimation of a corpse in the first century, but also about the possibility of Christ giving new life to people who were locked into some form of spiritual death now.

He told them the story of Raskolnikov, a character in Dostoevsky's *Crime and Punishment*, who had killed his own self in the act of murdering another person, but who had been brought back to life through the witness of these words in John's Gospel.

Afterwards a Marine corporal followed the chaplain to his cabin and, after a few faltering words, said: "Chaplain, I felt as though everything we read this morning was pointed right at me. I've been living in hell for the last six months, and for the first time I feel as though I'd gotten free."

As his story came out, it was the ordinary one of a boy in his teens thousands of miles from the supports and love of home who had gone further and further into sordid and self-destructive behavior, until at last, like the prodigal of Jesus' famous story, he had no self-respect and will to resist. Each day as his ship drew nearer to San Francisco, his guilt and despair had deepened into utter hopelessness.

"Up until today, Chaplain, I've been a dead man. I have felt utterly condemned by myself, by my family (if they knew), and by God. I've been dead, but now, after reading about Jesus and Lazarus, I know that I am alive again."

I believe in the actual resurrection of Christ. His was a real death, his mother's grief as deep as any mother's who turns from her child's new grave. And I believe that his resurrection was as real as his death and burial. God reversed the decision and the occasion became, not the end of his life, but its new beginning. "This Jesus God raised up, and of that we all are witnesses" (Acts 2:32), one of his friends declared shortly after the event.

To palm off some lame explanation that they sensed his spirit among them after his death or that they felt his continuing influence, is to do manifest violence to the Gospels' clear and explicit word. We may refuse to credit their claims, but we should not turn them into stories not meant to be taken quite seriously.

Christ's actual survival of the event of physical death becomes the Christian's warrant for believing that we also shall survive death. "Because I live, you will live also" (John 14:19*b*).

But there are other resurrections. We need not wait until that last death to discover the power of the resurrection. Whatever of yourself you need to reclaim from the death to which you have consigned it, reach out in the name and power of the resurrected Lord and claim it. In him is life. Through him we can move out of the shade and live in the sun.

2

The Other Side of Sunday

An eloquent black preacher captured the Easter truth in a Good Friday sermon which he punctuated with the refrain, "It's Friday. But Sunday's comin'!" Sunday has come, to be sure, but until you stand on the other side of it—the Friday side—the crucifixion side—you have no way of knowing the exhilaration of the resurrection. Unless you have known the shattering of hope brought about by Christ's death you can't know the joy of his resurrection.

What that preacher was creating for his congregation is the sense of desolation felt by the witnesses of Jesus' death. How can we moderns know the excitement of the message "He is risen!" unless we have really heard the crushing news, "He is dead"? We stand safely on this side of the cross and the empty tomb. Oh, we know that he was crucified, of course, but we know it in the light of his resurrection. We look at that dreadful occasion and say, "Christ died for our sins." But we don't stop there. "God raised him from the dead." To be sure. Ours is a resurrection faith. But in the process of witnessing to his resurrection we may deny that his death was real death.

We make his death less than dying. We turn the cross into a prop in a drama, his blood into tomato ketchup, and his executioners into friendly fellow actors who, as soon as the curtain falls, will help the crucified down from his uncomfortable position. "Christ died for our sins, but God raised him from the dead" becomes "All's well that ends well."

And it wasn't that way at all. There is no redemption in a ruse. Nobody is saved by a spoof. Jesus wasn't performing when he was nailed to the cross. What went on that day at Golgotha was not an act in a circus sideshow, like sawing the lady in a box in two. He didn't go home that night and talk to the Roman soldiers and his disciples about how they might make the performance more realistic. He died, period. He died in a cruel, horrible execution that must have turned strong men's stomachs to watch.

A modern scholar wrote convincingly about Jesus' life and ministry. But when he came to the crucifixion he took off in a flight of fancy. Jesus really didn't die at all, the scholar argued out of his imagination. What happened, he said, was that the "wine and gall" they gave him to drink while he was hanging on the cross was actually a concoction of drugs designed to knock him out and make him appear dead. It was all a pious fraud, said this debunker of the cross, set up ahead of time by Jesus and his friends. They came and took his body from the cross, by prearrangement putting him in Joseph's tomb until he "slept it off." When he came to, he got up and walked away. And that, said the scholar, was the resurrection.

If so, the Gospels are a deliberate lie. It is incredible that men and women would be transformed by a hoax they themselves had designed. The resurrection changed them from a frightened, hiding band into a courageous army. How shall we dismiss the grief and despair of the disciples after the Lord's death and before the news of his resurrection? Can we call their grief a hoax? One of the Gospels reports two men walking from Jerusalem to a village called Emmaus on the day of the resurrection. The men were among the grief-stricken. The events of that fateful Friday had shattered them. "We had hoped that he was the one to redeem Israel" (Luke 24:21), they said as they walked along disconsolately.

The New Testament writers were so jubilant about the resurrection because they experienced the defeat of Jesus' death. The first thing they wanted to tell other people about Jesus was not where or when or how he was born, or what he said and did, but that he was crucified and God raised him. Everything related to Christian faith revolved around that central event of his death and resurrection. It was the theme of early Christian preaching, the motivation of evangelism, and the reason for worship. Christians gathered to proclaim the living Lord, not to lay wreaths on the grave of a slain hero.

The impact of the resurrection was such that Paul compared it to the creation and fall of the human race. "For as in Adam all die," he wrote, "so also in Christ shall all be made alive" (1 Cor. 15:22). It was as though the world had been re-created.

It meant that God had intervened and taken a personal hand in our affairs. It gave dramatic witness to the fact that right had been vindicated by God's power. The grave injustice of the crucifixion, bringing what appeared to be a calamitous defeat to love and truth and everything good, had been reversed. The resurrection had cancelled the victory notices of evil.

The astonishing claim of these witnesses to Christ's resurrection was that the power which had brought him forth had been released in their own lives, that God had indeed raised them to newness of life—but also that they looked forward to bodily resurrection.

But before Sunday was Friday, before the resurrection, the crucifixion. The resurrection is a miracle only because the crucifixion was a reality.

3

Don't Give Up on Hope

People can endure pain, poverty, hunger, oppression, and a multitude of other assaults upon human dignity, but they cannot long live without hope. Hope is indispensable to life and health. Dark despair, unrelieved by hope's light, will make you sick. Stare too long into the blackness and you lose the capacity to look at the light.

Is hope then a mere accommodation in order to remain sane? Is enjoyment of hopefulness the pay-off for swallowing hard and telling yourself that things are not as bad as you know they are? Is hope the result of a deliberate decision to reside in a make-believe world of cotton candy and brightly colored lights? Are the hopeful those too dumb to be depressed?

Some of my counselees think so. They are so miserable that they cannot understand how an intelligent person could have hope. They imagine themselves to be the true realists. Their own world has fallen apart. How dare anyone with intelligence be anything but despairing?

I tell them that the Bible is both realistic and hopeful. Oh, how realistic a Book it is! In fact, some people have trouble with its realism. The Bible pulls no punches about the folly of our human striving. It paints us accurately, "warts and all." Nothing of our seaminess is omitted. Adultery, incest, murder, rape, theft, brutality, greed, oppression, idolatry—you name it, it is all there in the Bible. And over that sordid mess is the possibility for human glory as children of God.

With all that, what a Book of hope the Bible is! Get your Bible down and read Psalm 42. Let the writer of that hymn share his dark forebodings with you.

> My soul thirsts for God. . . .
> My tears have been my food day and night.
> These things I remember
>   as I pour out my soul:

> how I went with the throng,
>> and led them in procession to the house of God . . .
> Why are you cast down, O my soul? . . .
> Hope in God; for I shall again praise him,
>> my help and my God (vv. 2-6).

That man knew about depression, yet he never gave up hope. He remembered times when he had felt close to God when he had "led . . . the procession to the house of God" (Ps. 42:4). He clung to that memory. The closeness had vanished, but he would not deny that the closeness had been real, or tell himself that it was more honest and noble to be depressed. He clung to the hope he had once known, confident that he would come to it again.

Turn to the New Testament and you will see that it, too, is about hope. The central figure of the New Testament was executed on a Roman cross. The bottom fell out for Jesus' followers that awful day of his death. He had warned them, but they were so caught up in the exhilaration of his movement that they could not hear. When they saw him die, they thought it was all over. Their hope was crushed.

News of his resurrection took them totally by surprise. When women ran, bursting into their hiding place to announce that he was risen "the apostles," writes Luke, "thought that what the women said was nonsense, and they did not believe them" (24:11, GNB).

But they found to their utter amazement that, indeed, it was true. Christ is alive, returned from death! That message became the basis of all their hope, for his death had been the worst thing that could ever happen. Darkness had made its ultimate move against light and, as John put it, "the light is still shining" (John 1:5, author's translation).

In his letter to the Romans, Paul writes about the source and nature of hope. Hope, he says, is not the naive assumption that life will never go sour. Hope is not a magic spray applied like one's favorite deodorant. It is what is left after the test of fire, the pure metal when the alloy has been burned out.

Hope for the Christian, Paul wrote, is not based upon a natural disposition toward optimism. It is the end result of a life process. The process is a cycle of affliction (meaning "pressure")—endurance—character—hope. You never learn to endure without experiencing pressure. You can't get in shape without having a case of shin splints and sore muscles. Nor do you develop character without learning how to endure. Character is developed from "keeping on keeping on." When you have come that far, you then know something about hope.

This hope is not the product of a well-adusted personality or of a fortunate endocrine system. Hope emerges from the trials of affliction if you have faith in God. If you trust God who brought Jesus forth from the dead, then you can afford to hope even in the midst of darkness.

4

The Son Who Was Not Spared

Long ago lived a God-fearing man named Abraham with his wife Sarah. Parenthood came late to them, but after long and disappointing years of waiting, a son was born. They named him "Isaac," which means "Laughter." Did the name say something of the hopes and dreams they had for this boy?

No little child is ordinary to his parents, but perhaps, because he had come so late and was the only one, they lavished more love on him than was usual. However, there really was something special about this lad. Abraham was a man of destiny. God had dealings with him, had rooted him out of his home country, and sent him westward to a new land with the promise to make him the father of a great nation through which all the families of the earth would be blessed.

It sounded incredible, but here Abraham was far from his native land and people, living in a tent in a country which he had been assured his posterity would possess. And was not the little boy the assurance of posterity—this little tousle-haired fellow following him around, idolizing him, believing he was the strongest, bravest, truest man who ever lived? Wasn't Isaac all the proof Abraham needed that God is as good as his word?

Then one day a deep shadow fell across Abraham's face and sorrow darkened his eyes. With woman's intuition Sarah knew that something had gone wrong, but she couldn't pull it out of him. He shrugged off her questions and kept the dread secret locked up in his heart until he thought it would burst open someday when he was playing with his boy.

One night as "Laughing Boy" lay sleeping near them on his pallet, his still little face like an angel's, Abraham could bear it no longer and brought the awful thing out and shared it with his wife. God who had made the promise, God who had given the child, now demanded that Abraham give the child back. He was to take Isaac and offer him as a human sacrifice on the holy mountain, Moriah, killing his own son as an act of obedience to God.

Surely Abraham did not wait many days after that. There is a doom which delay only renders more frightful. Donkeys were saddled, food prepared, wood gathered, fire taken (no matches, remember). Only those who have taken perilous journeys or been separated from someone deeply loved, can know what Abraham and Sarah felt that day.

Whom shall we pity more, the mother sobbing alone at the entrance to her tent, watching a happy, expectant little figure retreating into the distance, or Abraham suddenly grown old with the weight of an unbearable burden?

It must have been an eternity to Abraham before they came to the place on the third day. "Stay here," said the father to his servants. "The boy and I will go up yonder and worship and come back to you." And with that overpowering simplicity of the Bible the story says: "So they went both of them together."

When they came to the top of the mountain the lad missed the sacrifice. "Here is the wood and here is the fire," he said, "but where is the lamb?" (see Gen. 22:7). And all that Abraham could manage was to say with choking voice, "The Lord will provide." He would spare the boy the terror as long as he could.

Who can tell how Abraham managed those last moments? With what resources was he able to tie his boy to the improvised altar? Who raised Abraham's trembling arm above his son's breast bared for the knife's fatal plunge?

At that last split second before irreversible tragedy, there was the sound of a voice arresting the upraised arm, and the sight of a ram caught in the thicket. With hands fumbling at the ropes seen with eyes blinded by tears, Abraham untied his boy, sacrificed the ram, and came on back down the mountain with Isaac. And one wonders if "Laughing Boy" ever laughed again.

Perhaps this story was included in the Bible to remind God's people of the horror of child sacrifice. The Hebrews loved and cared for their children with rare devotion. But the story of "the son who was spared" reminds Christians of another event.

It is the event of "the Son who was not spared." Two thousand years after Abraham another young man was brought to the same kind of place. He was beaten and reviled. Then they killed him, nailing him to a cross.

As men reflected upon what had happened to this Son, Jesus Christ, they spoke in wonder of the love of the Father for sinful man. This is the way Paul, the New Testament's most gifted writer, put it: "He who did not spare his own Son, but gave him up for us all, will he not also give us all things with him?" (Rom. 8:32).

II
A Future and a Hope

1

Tough times bring out either the best or the worst in us. A people threatened may respond by losing its will and resign itself to presumed historical necessity, or it may arouse itself to unusual, even heroic, endeavor. We may behave like looters, taking advantage of disaster to pillage, or we may unselfishly spend our strength and ingenuity to overcome the effects of catastrophe. Which we decide to be and do is not so much a matter of the head as of the heart. A people without will, without hope, without leadership, dooms itself to mediocrity and meaninglessness.

Such a peril and such a choice confront us. The structure of our social order is threatened by forces we did not altogether create, but which we must learn to manage else they will destroy us. Inflation, energy, deficit spending, militarism, welfare, a spreading and creeping bureaucracy—are the dread names we give to our dangers.

But they are not our gravest peril. That is the loss of heart and will, the loss of confidence in the possibility that government can be more than self-serving, the loss of faith in ourselves, and the loss of trust in one another. "We have met the enemy, and he is us," commented the late Walt Kelly's "Pogo." We are an endangered species if we cease to believe.

What kind of people are we? Do we have the heart and will to create a strong, equitable, decent society in which we care about one another, care about the quality of our public education and of the environment, care about the poor, the elderly, and the disadvantaged, care that people have work to do and care about the quality of the work that is done?

A remarkable incident in the history of ancient Israel twenty-six centuries ago is appropriate to this occasion. Judah and her proud capital, Jerusalem, had fallen to the Babylonians, her leading citizens taken captive. The nation reeled under the shock of crushing defeat, its leadership gone, its cities laid waste, its economy destroyed. They had refused to believe that it could happen, despite the warnings of the prophet Jeremiah. But it had happened, and the nation's leadership was removed to Babylon.

The prophets and advisors to the court, that customary crew of motley, self-serving yes-people whom the Bible dismisses as false prophets, went along with the king to Babylon. There they set up business as usual, making shallow pronouncements about the "state of the state." "This is nothing serious," they reassured the people. "God is going to bring us back to Jerusalem within two years, and the captivity will be only a bad dream."

When Jeremiah heard about these verbal placebos, he wrote a letter to the exiles. The letter exudes with confidence in God's ultimate purpose for the well-being of his people, but it is also full of direct, plain-spoken encouragement to the people to match their crisis with their best efforts. "God plans to give you a future and a hope," Jeremiah wrote.

But there was more to it than that. First, Jeremiah wrote that they should not listen to the people who claimed there was no serious crisis. Don't look for easy answers to hard questions, he declared. The fair-weather prophets would advise you to relax and take it easy. People are always intrigued by the easy answer. It is terribly tempting to governments to over-promise. We have victimized ourselves in this country by encouraging aspirants for public office to out-promise one another. That leads inevitably to disillusionment and cynicism when government cannot deliver.

Jeremiah's second word to the exiles was: they should settle down and do what they could where they were. The way to the future is to be faithful to your present responsibilities. Build houses; plant gardens; settle down; unpack your bags; marry and give your children in marriage. The normal processes of life must go on. Do what you can, and do your best. Avoid the "interim mentality" which is always looking somewhere else for the meaning of existence.

The prophet's third word to the exiles was to get involved in the life of Babylon. Those inclined to feel that they had no stake in the well-being of the country are urged to participate. "Seek the welfare of the city where I have sent you into exile, and pray to the Lord on its behalf, for in its welfare you will find your welfare" (Jer. 29:7). It is still good advice. Get involved; be a participant; care about your community.

The final word to the exiles is that God has not forgotten where they are. He has plans for you, Jeremiah wrote, plans to give you a future and a hope. But the exiles must want it with all their hearts. God is not to be had by the uncommitted and the uncaring. "You will seek me and find me," God says, "when you seek me with all your heart" (v. 13).

2

Does Religion Really Matter?

In a sermon preached years ago at the Madison Avenue Presbyterian Church, New York, Dr. David H. C. Read quoted a provocative sentence from Gibbon's classic study, *The Decline and Fall of the Roman Empire*. The historian had written: "The various modes of worship which prevailed in the Roman world were all considered by the people as equally true; by the philosophers as equally false, and by the magistrates as equally useful."

What a frightening indictment of any society—all religions judged by the people to be equally true, by the philosophers equally false, and by the politicians equally useful! Will historians reflecting upon latter twentieth-century America render a similar verdict?

The Roman world was full of religious objects—temples, shrines, idols, synagogues. For instance, when the apostle Paul came to

Athens, he said to her citizens, "I perceive that in every way you are very religious" (Acts 17:22). Would he not say the same of your city, with a church or synagogue on every corner?

But the people were indiscriminate about religion. All were equally valid. If a little religion is good, a lot is better. If you are in doubt about the ability of one god, consult another oracle. So one living in the first century might be a devotee at a half-dozen altars.

That is a common sight today. In the name of broadmindedness people wander from church to church, sampling here and there, seeking satisfying noninvolvement, which is really a contradiction in terms. There is a growing cult of the unidentified in America. They think all churches are nice, and everybody is trying to go to heaven, but since no church is exactly what they are looking for they settle on none.

Multitudes of others go so far as to join a religious group but their commitment is so meaningless as to make no difference. Their "religions" are many: work, having fun, collecting things, admiring their bodies or taking care of them, or a hundred others. Like the Athenians, they are very religious, but church is one of the least important shrines. They hardly know the way to its doors.

Is not the second group cited by the historian, the philosophers who considered all religions as equally false, well represented in our society, too? The intellectuals, the sophisticates were quite willing for the unlearned, common people to have their myths and folklore. It helped ease the pain of their suffering and relieve the drabness of everyday life. But the "thinking man" couldn't have cared less. All religions equally false!

Ours is a culture nearly totally secularized now. The fantastic scientific breakthroughs of the past few decades threaten the patterns of religious thought and expression. Why worry about God or another existence after death when such exciting things are happening right around us? What can the preacher promise that the scientist hasn't made look like child's play?

Besides, the religious people have not solved the perplexing problems of our society. They have frequently escaped dealing with the problems by concentrating on being "religious." Sometimes they have even arrayed themselves against the solution of problems and have done so in the name of being religious.

We who believe that our religion has to do with all of life, that there is no ultimate meaning apart from our faith, ought not to underestimate the impact of this intellectual revolution in our day. It is the plain fact that many a thoughtful person has dismissed religion as irrelevant.

But what of the third group mentioned by Gibbon? Do we have their counterparts—those who viewed all religions as equally useful? Yes, regretfully we do. These are the people who identify religion with whatever cause they espouse. Their real concern is the thing they promote. Religion is dragged in to sanctify the effort, but such a procedure scarcely conceals the fact that religion is being used as a means rather than being a worthy end in itself.

This is not to suggest, of course, that faith in God is dissociated from the issues of life. It is to say that to love God first with all one's being is the only escape from idolatry. Just because we do love God we are called to relate every area of life to his prior claim upon us.

Do you fit into either of Gibbon's three categories? If so, religion really does not matter to you!

3

Free At Last! Free At Last!

As the hostages filed out of the Algiers airport building and strolled toward the waiting American planes, looking more like tired Friday-night commuters than subjects of global controversy and concern, I mainly felt relief. "Are all fifty-two accounted for?" some commentator asked. "Has anybody seen So-and-so, or So-and-so?" Yes, they were all present and accounted for, we were assured.

Despite enthusiastic handshakes and fulsome compliments exchanged by American and Algerian diplomats, everybody wanted to be sure that there had been no last-minute surprises. With a rush of gratitude and relief we were reassured. The fourteen-month vigil was ending. The monstrous illegal act of imprisoning innocent citizens of another sovereign nation in defiance of all international law had concluded with last-minute arranged mob-scene verbal abuse of the Americans even as they walked to the Algerian planes at Tehran. But it was over now. To paraphrase Martin Luther King's rousing words: "Free at last! Free at last! Great God Almighty, we're (they're) free at last!"

By the time this becomes newsprint we may know more about the private thoughts of those fifty-two Americans as they sat quietly waiting in the Algiers airport. There were few signs of jubilation. Hearty handshakes, words of appreciation to the Algerian diplomats who acted as intermediaries, were seen, but nobody was dancing in the streets. Did the last hour seem longest, or had they learned not to count time by hours during the long months of separation from their families? In any event, one of them, mounting the steps to the American plane, turned and shouted before disappearing through the door, "God bless America!" Amen and amen.

It is an irony of history that some of our biblical forebears were held hostage 2,500 years ago in a city called Babylon, in a region not far from Tehran, Iran. That captivity lasted, not fourteen months, but more than half a century! It is another piece of historical irony that those Jewish forebears of ours were set free by the forebears of the same Iranians who held our people in bondage. In the year 539 BC, Cyrus the Persian overthrew Babylon, and soon thereafter issued an edict releasing all Babylonian hostages to return to their homeland.

Most of the Jewish hostages in Babylon had never seen Jerusalem. They had only heard about its glory from their parents who lived and died in Babylon singing:

> If I forget you, O Jerusalem,
>   let my right hand wither!
> Let my tongue cleave to the roof of my mouth,
>   if I do not remember you,
> if I do not set Jerusalem
>   above my highest joy! (Ps. 137:5-6).

A Future and a Hope / 29

Imbued with such passionate devotion to the homeland, Jews who had known only Babylon eagerly made the 600-mile pilgrimage to Jerusalem. One of the most powerful sections of the Bible was written to celebrate that homecoming. It begins with Isaiah 40 in which an inspired poet writes:

> A voice cries:
> "In the wilderness prepare the way of the Lord,
>   make straight in the desert a highway for our God" (v. 3).

No hill would seem too high, no valley too low. The uneven ground would be as though level, and the rough places would be like a plain. With wings on their feet and the wind at their backs, the prisoners were marching home.

To the poet it seemed that even nature rejoiced in the liberation. Listen:

> For you shall go out in joy,
>   and be led forth in peace;
> the mountains and the hills before you
>   shall break forth into singing,
>   and all the trees of the field shall clap their hands (Isa. 55:12).

What a lovely picture of delight!

It was not only a time to march, and a time to rejoice, but also a time to proclaim. Let the world know what the Lord has done. Tell everybody about the liberation. Listen:

> The Spirit of the Lord God is upon me,
>   because the Lord has anointed me
> to bring good tidings to the afflicted;
>   he has sent me to bind up the broken-hearted,
> to proclaim liberty to the captives,
>   and the opening of the prison to those who are bound"
>   (61:1; see also Luke 4:18).

In his inaugural sermon, the Lord Jesus Christ took his text from those words of Isaiah. He had come to proclaim a liberation of the hostages. He had come to live and die that all persons might be set free to return to their Father's home.

There is a bondage more dehumanizing than physical imprisonment. There is a captivity worse than Babylonian or Iranian. It is slavery to selfishness, meanness of spirit, contempt and hatred for others, fear and despair. In short, the worst of all bondages is the bondage to sin.

Some sin bondage is obvious. We see a person bound in cruel chains of drug or alcohol abuse, and we do not have to be told that that is slavery. We see one bound in the chains of ignorance and we want to set him free. Do we recognize the subtler and more destructive forms of bondage in which all of us struggle? Christ came to set us free. As he said: "So if the Son makes you free, you will be free indeed" (John 8:36).

4

Between Suicide and Slavery

A relative just back from China was talking about the startling contrast he noted between the People's Republic of China, a totalitarian state, and the excesses of the free city of Hong Kong sitting right off the coast of China.

Hong Kong struck him as the epitome of all that is ugly in Western culture. The widening gap between haves and have-nots is nowhere more dramatically seen. Rolls-Royce and Mercedes limos whiz through streets clogged with pushcarts, and honk impatiently at pedestrians impeding their way. Palatial mansions stand out garishly against the background of tarpaper and corrugated metal shacks. Staggering wealth and mind-boggling poverty coexist. Glittering neon signs, massage parlors, prostitution, drugs, and wide-open pornography are the tawdry confirmations of the worst that the totalitarians can say about democracy.

A few miles away, on the mainland, the picture is totally different. Streets, kept clean of garbage and debris by human sweepers with brooms made of brush, are teeming with people racially very much like the people of Hong Kong. There the similarity ends. The forced egalitarianism of a totalitarian state produces a spectacle of masses of look-alikes in dress and behavior. There is no unemployment, everybody is eating, and there is no public display of sexual exploitation. Neither is there any public dissent. Even the "freedom wall," where protests against public policy once were posted, is no more. One has the impression, my informant observed, freedom has been exchanged for security.

Are freedom or security mankind's only options? "Give me liberty or give me death," Patrick Henry shouted in Saint John's Church in Richmond, Virginia, in 1775, when the American Revolution was brewing. But as someone has commented, "Why does the first so often lead to the second?" Must liberty always lead to excess, and excess to self-destruction? Must man always be reduced to choosing between slavery and suicide?

I submit that this is the basic human dilemma. Here is illustrated what the late David E. Roberts called "the grandeur and misery of man." He cherishes freedom but appears rarely able to sustain it for long by the kind of self-restraint which makes it viable. He resists others' regulating him, but discovers lamentably too late that the unregulated life is self-destructive. The unpoliced community faces either anarchy or oppression.

What is happening in the United States today? People are arming themselves, dead-bolting their doors, installing sophisticated burglar-alarm systems, and hiring private security guards to watch their neighborhoods. The other day I sat at a table with about twenty homeowners who were meeting about a matter totally incidental to the question of personal security. When someone mentioned that his house had been burglarized over the holidays, it turned out that nearly everyone around the table had experienced that unnerving intrusion.

The simple fact is that in some societies thieves have their hands chopped off. We Americans, myself included, are horrified by such barbaric punishment for crimes against property. But is it improper to raise the question about the alternatives to either barbarism or anarchy?

As a college chaplain I see daily this dilemma acted out in the lives of young people. Our college, although the students do not think so, permits a large degree of freedom in matters concerning choice of life-style. Most of our young people do quite well exercising responsible self-restraint. They live decent, God-fearing lives. They are good citizens in the dormitory and classroom. But, frankly, some students are unable to manage freedom. They lack self-discipline; lacking it they commit academic suicide or self-destruct in other ways.

This is the dilemma. Which shall it be? Hong Kong style or mainland China style? Do we have to force people to dress alike, think alike, behave alike, in order to keep them from the excesses that end in death?

I like Kentucky Coach Joe Hall's explanation when questioned about his action of suspending two star players right before an important basketball game. He said he did it because they persisted in breaking well-established training rules. "Where there is no discipline," he said, "you soon have anarchy." I say amen.

III
Making the Living Worthwhile

1

An old boy I appreciate used to kid his wife by saying when he introduced her, "She makes the living and I make the living worthwhile." I always figured he was exaggerating on both counts, but there sure is more to life than making a living. It ought to be worthwhile.

Fall is just about here, and after whatever vacation you got, it's back to the desk, to the bench, or to the line. The children will be catching the school bus and complaining about homework again, and you will be yelling at them to turn down the stereo or cut off the TV. What makes the living worthwhile?

This week I saw the results of a questionnaire answered by 17,000 high school graduates of this past June. Of the things rated by this group of young Americans as "extremely important," the No. 1 item is "a good marriage and family life." Maybe our young people are not as decadent as they have been thought to be. "Strong friendships" was the second most important thing in life to those heading for college. Also extremely important to the high school graduates, whether going to college or not, are "finding purpose and meaning in my life," "Finding steady work," and "Being successful in my work."

I don't know, of course, if the people who responded to the questionnaire are representative of the eighteen-year-olds of this country, although it would seem that 17,000 is a fair sample. But the values they espouse sound pretty good to me.

One of the striking things about these answers is the expectations of the high school graduates when contrasted with the actualities as experienced by their parents. The overwhelming and distressing evidence is that Americans are not terribly happy in either their marriages or their work. Maybe the difference is nothing more significant than the difference between being eighteen and forty-five.

In any case, I believe that what makes the living worthwhile is connected to the sense of vocation. *Vocation* is a fancy word for the feeling that you are where you are supposed to be and doing what you can do well. If you are not experiencing that, it won't matter how much they pay you or whether you are living with your spouse. What makes you feel good about yourself is a sense of vocation.

As a Christian I believe that vocation, or calling, is related to your attitude toward God. If you really believe that God is personally involved in your life and that what you do or don't do pleases or disappoints him, it puts the entire matter in a different light. If my marriage and my work are somehow connected to the plans and hopes of the Almighty to create in the human family a kingdom of God, then it is worthwhile, however humble or however hard.

The Scriptures say a lot about calling. Our biblical forebears were crystal clear at this point. They saw themselves as a people of destiny, the chosen. They did not always enjoy the role, and they often repudiated it by their behavior. Sometimes they were guilty of misinterpreting and abusing their call. But the sense of vocation runs like a purple thread through the story of Israel and of the New Testament church.

This conviction that they weren't out there in the world by themselves provided the drive and force of the early Christians. So, for example, the apostle Paul writes to his young protégé, Timothy: "Stir up the gift of God which is in thee. . . . For God hath not given us the spirit of fear; but of power, and of love, and of a sound mind" (2 Tim. 1:6-7, KJV).

We do not know what prompted the admonition. Was Timothy beginning to drift into some mid-career crisis? Had he gotten weary of catching grain ships to the next town, or walking long, hot days, to preach the gospel? Was he resting on his laurels, deceiving himself by taking his press clippings too seriously? We do not know. What we do know is that Paul saw him as letting the fire of his vocation go out. He needed to agitate the smouldering coals before they turned into black cinders.

There is plenty of common sense in what Paul wrote to Timothy. If you are drifting along without much purpose and with no sense of accomplishment in your life, then what you are doing isn't very worthwhile to you. It probably wouldn't help to change your address or spouse or job, but a change of attitude would do wonders. Reach down within yourself to the bedrock of your conviction about the meaning of your life. Is God trying to do something with you and for you and by you? If so, then life is worth living.

2

Looking for Salvage

Ever daydream of finding a buried and long-forgotten treasure chest full of Spanish doubloons and jewels? Ever want to join a crew of adventurers exploring the floor of the ocean for wrecked hulks of ships that went down with huge treasures aboard? Would you like to help raise the *Titanic?*

Could you get excited about finding an old, beat-up piece of furniture, the natural beauty of its wood hidden beneath coat after coat of garish paint, and restoring it to its original loveliness? I envy a friend's talent. He restores and drives antique automobiles.

Despite our American "throwaway" mentality, something deeper —and finer—in most of us responds to the opportunity to reclaim, rather than discard, things of value. We were brainwashed to accept a plastic culture. Nonreturnable bottles and plastic cups may at last bury us if we are not first choked to death in bureaucratic paper.

"Throwaway" mentality affects a huge segment of our corporate life. That is what is happening to marriage, for instance. The epidemic of marriage-divorce-marriage is simply another way of expressing the attitude that, once used, a thing or a relationship is of no further value to you. So you discard it and get another, like reaching for a second paper cup, rather than realistically seeing what can be done to make the old relationship shine with the luster of renewal.

But there is one person you cannot discard—yourself. If the Bible is true, you will never be somebody else, only yourself. As individual as your fingerprints is your own person and you can't get yourself off your hands. You can't dump yourself on somebody else, or do away with yourself. Death is not the end of you, the Bible says. Even in the torment of hell there is self-consciousness. Indeed, one must wonder if self-consciousness and self-loathing are hell's worst torments.

If it is true that nothing is ever finished about us, that all is in process, that we have not become but are becomers, then the salvage business is one we ought to know something about. We would not need to know about human salvage operations if we never needed salvaging. If we moved from victory to victory and success to success, there would be no occasion to think about recovery. If failure were an unknown word in our vocabulary, we would have no need of salvage.

Since you cannot trade yourself in for a new model, what do you do when you face the fact that the present model is in bad need of repair? That is where we Christians have something to say. Ours is a religion that presupposes the continual need for repair. The church is not a showroom full of shiny, brand-new models. It is a garage full of grimy, beat-up, broken-down used cars in various stages of reclamation.

The Bible, Old as well as New Testament, has much to say about how God comes to our aid in this project. My favorite verse on this subject is Romans 8:28. There are numerous translations of it, in part because there are several variations of the Greek text of the verse, but the one which speaks to my condition reads: "We know that in everything God works for good with those who love him, who are called according to his purpose."

Please notice that the verse does not contend that "everything is for the best." A great many people draw comfort from that reading of the verse, but I can't. If it consoles you to believe that, no matter how horrendous the events which tear up your life, it is all God's will and for the best, I wouldn't want to take that consolation away from you.

But I must tell you that I am not helped by the thought that God has sent some of the tragedies I have witnessed.

It is great consolation, however, to know that in whatever happens I have God's good offices on my side. But could God not prevent these terrible things from happening? Of course he could. Then why doesn't he? I am not sure I can answer that question. Maybe it would mess up his system and destroy our chances for spiritual and intellectual maturity if he took over our care like a hovering parent over her toddler. We are going to fall down and hurt ourselves plenty of times while learning to walk. It is that kind of world.

But what this verse says is that when we do he is there to help us pick ourselves up and try again. I can't speak for you, but I find tremendous solace and encouragement in that. And I have experienced it. This is one area in which I can write from experience.

So, to all who have shipwrecked some of their finest ideals and hopes, to all who have suffered what looks like irreparable damage, to all who think that life has consigned them to the discard pile, I write this word of encouragement. There is wondrous beauty in your life, and God the Master Workman is eager to help you salvage it.

3

Balancing the New and Old

Last weekend was homecoming at our university, and the campus was alive with the happy sounds of reunion. People who had graduated fifty years ago mingled with freshmen in the dining hall. I couldn't resist thinking about how both groups—old and new—have common causes and are involved with one another. The scene made me remember that everyone's life is made up of the new and the old.

Mature persons are both innovators and conservers. They maintain their zest for discovery but do not disdain treasure already found. Some people make great researchers; they will try anything once.

Other are competent curators; they know a good thing when they see it. The trick is being both, and there is an art to it.

It is perilously easy to separate the two parts of learning/living. Think, for instance, how preoccupied we are with novelty. Hucksters hawk their wares in terms of the irresistibility of newness. Whether it be detergent, breakfast food, or underarm deodorant, its reason for being is that it is "new and improved."

We have built an economy based upon planned obsolescence. How could you possibly be so gauche as to wear last year's styles? And anyone who drives an old model automobile is publicly declaring that he is a failure. And serial marriage is now nearly standard for Americans who can afford to change partners every few years. After all, should one deny oneself the exhilaration of a new mate?

The Bible shares the universal longing for newness. "In the sweet bye and bye" is a song native to Scripture. It keeps pointing to the future: "One day things will be better." "When we get to the Promised Land." "When the end comes. . . ."

"I saw a new heaven and a new earth," wrote John in the Revelation. "If anyone is in Christ," wrote Paul, "he is a new creation." I suspect that everyone shares the hope of finding new treasure, of closing the door on whatever is painful about the past and turning toward some bright future.

But, of course, that can't happen. No matter where you go you take your baggage. It fills not only your car trunk but also your mind and heart. You have to learn to sort it, separate it, discard some and keep what is worth preserving.

Jesus put this graphically in one of his brief parables: "Therefore every scribe who has been trained for the kingdom of heaven is like a householder who brings out of his treasure what is new and what is old" (Matt. 13:52).

The parable intrigues me, in part because Jesus was clearly drawing upon his own religious heritage. Scribes were experts, schoolmen. They had a Ph.D. in religion! But their training was largely in the lore of their religious past.

Notice that Jesus did not decry that kind of learning; it was only that he saw it as incomplete. One trained for his kingdom, the kingdom of heaven, had another dimension. His storehouse held both new and old things.

Further, the parable interests me because of the way Jesus put the two together—first the new, then the old. I am sure that I would have arranged them in reverse order, but he was a better student of human nature.

The "new" is always more glittering. After all, it is new, and catches our attention first. We have to be infatuated with novelty and then discover that it won't work all the time and must be revised and supplemented by the ancient truth we temporarily set aside.

If you are old enough to have a history worth talking about, you know this from experience. The measure of your maturity is the skill you have developed in balancing the new and the old.

Jesus' insight is that neither is adequate to provide sound bases for life. We need both in the family, the community, and the nation. And we need both in our individual lives.

But some folks suppose that you cannot have both in the individual. They think that the immaturity of youth is preoccupation with novelty, while the bane of old age is its irrational devotion to the past. They suppose that the function of each group is to correct the imbalance of the other.

Jesus had a better idea. Whatever your age, learn to value both the new and the old treasure. That is genuine maturity.

IV
What Is There to Be Grateful About?

1

In the measure that gratitude is missing, character is flawed. Without gratitude the privileged become proud and self-sufficient, if not arrogant and intolerant. And without gratitude the underprivileged become absorbed in self-pity, if not in cynicism and despair. Gratitude is the saving salt that both preserves life and makes it palatable.

A little-known book of the Old Testament, Habakkuk, puts the issue of thankfulness in clear perspective. Written in the twilight decades of Judah's independence just before the darkness of Babylonian Captivity, the prophecy raises the question of undeserved suffering and God's silence:

> O Lord, how long shall I cry for help,
>   and thou wilt not hear? . . .
> Thou who art of purer eyes than to behold evil
>   and canst not look on wrong,
> why dost thou look on faithless men,
>   and art silent when the wicked swallows up
>   the man more righteous than he?" (Hab. 1:2*a*,13).

Doubtless you have felt like Habakkuk. The Lord answered the prophet somewhat as follows: "I understand your impatience, Habakkuk, but you must take a longer look than your own day and generation. Sometimes God's people have to wait for his work to be done. Waiting is tedious, but remember that the just shall live by his faithfulness."

But the promise of future correction of injustice, pie in the sky by-and-by, was small comfort to the prophet whose world was falling apart. "O Lord," he lamented "I have heard reports of your former doings, and I am impressed. But in this present crisis we need something more substantial than tales about the good old days, or promises of future action. Sir, renew Thy work in the midst of the years—do it now!" (3:2, author's translation).

If Habakkuk lived long enough, he discovered that the Lord was able to be in Babylon as well as in Jerusalem. But in the meantime, there was nothing to do but wait. Thus his prophecy comes to an end with a strong affirmation of the true nature of gratitude:

> Though the fig tree do not blossom,
>   nor fruit be on the vines,
> the produce of the olive fail
>   and the fields yield no food,
> the flock be cut off from the fold
>   and there be no herd in the stalls,
> yet I will rejoice in the Lord,
>   I will joy in the God of my salvation" (3:17-18).

That is a fine summation of the "great nevertheless." Only as we can be thankful "in spite of" and not "because of" do we experience the meaning of gratitude.

Gratitude does not arise out of being healthy, wealthy, and wise, or from marrying the boss or the boss's daughter. If that were true, the people who enjoy such benefits would be unfailingly thankful, and the have-nots uniformly thankless. Nothing in experience supports such a reading of life. Here is a fundamental issue. The source of gratitude is in one's basic understanding of existence, not in the size of one's house, or bank account, or the horsepower under the hood. We have to have some more substantial reason for gratitude than the fact that we never had it so good, else thankfulness is a fair-weather, occasional thing.

Neither is the source of gratitude to be found in comparative wellbeing. Don't deceive yourself into being thankful merely because you do not have somebody else's problems. That nearly always leads to self-congratulation, saying with the Pharisee in Jesus' parable: "God, I thank thee that I am not as other men are" (Luke 18:11, KJV).

A poster advertising a campaign for funds to fight crippling diseases of children featured a child in a wheelchair with the caption: "Be thankful you can walk." Being able to walk is indeed something to be thankful for, but can such thankfulness be properly based upon the realization that others cannot? Shall I respond to my awareness of others' distress by thanking God that I am not in distress? Shall my gratitude rise upon the winds of my neighbor's adversity?

Whence comes gratitude? It comes in the realization that all life is a gift from God. Thanksgiving is the purest form of worship. It arises from the realization of our incompleteness, brokenness, and insufficiency. Gratitude is that grace which enables us to accept dependency without resentment, to acknowledge life's givenness without surrendering our dignity or turning into arrogant eccentrics. Gratitude comes from the recognition that we are guests. Thankfulness presupposes that there is Someone to whom you should and may say thank you!

But what keeps thanksgiving from being an exercise in self-congratulation, or a form of fatalism which, when things go wrong, says with a shrug, "That's the way the cookie crumbles"? What keeps it from being perverted is a sense of our mutual obligation? What prevents it from being a pious binge in the name of turkey and pumpkin pie is the acknowledgment of both the vertical and horizontal planes of our existence? God's grace to me obligates me to his other children. If I have been especially blessed, I must seek especially to be a blessing.

2

He Sent Leanness

One of the most frequent impressions I get from talking to people is that they feel helpless to do anything significant about anything important. The feeling may be described as a sense of moral impotence. In a ministers' meeting one man said with a note of frustration and rage in his voice, "We are eunuchs serving this culture!"

What Is There to Be Grateful About / 43

Our condition may not be unlike that described by the psalmist in recounting Israel's history. Referring to the period of their aimless wandering in the wilderness for forty years, the poet wrote: "They soon forgat his works; they waited not for his counsel: But lusted exceedingly in the wilderness, and tempted God in the desert. And he gave them their request; but sent leanness into their soul" (Ps. 106:13-15, KJV).

The possibility that God has decided to let us wander without purpose or direction in this generation is disturbing. We have been phenomenally successful in producing a materialistic and pleasure-saturated culture. We have "lusted" after the comfortable life which a technological society can create. And God has not denied us our wishes.

But, oh, the leanness, the loneliness, the meaninglessness! Is leanness of soul the price of fatness of head and obesity of body? If so, is it a good trade-off, or have we shortchanged ourselves?

"We are the hollow men, we are the stuffed men, leaning together, headpiece filled with straw," wrote T. S. Eliot. The words are hauntingly in touch with our time and communicate a disturbingly familiar sense of the vacuum of meaninglessness in which many Americans are living.

Most of the persons who read a column like this are as conspicuous among the world's people as the factory owner living in a mansion surrounded by block after block of tar-paper shacks. Yet we are not conspicuous for being happy, integrated persons who are competent to make the whole community better for all who live in it, and are also committed to do just that.

Before his death Walter Lippmann wrote with an intense concern about the "loss of a sense of great purpose and high destiny" by the American people. And Elton Trueblood, now retired in Richmond, Indiana, called our national affliction a "loss of zest," saying that "our incentive is unequal to our skill." If it is true that we know how to do better than we are doing, then perhaps the word of the psalmist has come upon us—we got the desires of our hearts, but we also got "leanness of the soul."

How does it happen that with a billion hungry people in the world my chief health problem is obesity? Have I got a fat belly because I have a lean soul? If so, how come that combination?

Maybe we have paraded one value system too long while living by another. We have preached about caring, but we have not cared. We say that the essence of godliness is sharing, but our real priorities are not much different from a base, unredeemed drive for preserving and pleasuring ourselves.

We have talked to ourselves so much about how generous we are, how others feed off of us and then are ungrateful for our generosity, that we have come to believe our own propaganda. We say, "America can't feed the whole world." I was shocked to learn recently that the United States stands twelfth or thirteenth among the nations of the world in the percentage of its gross national produce given to feed the world. We currently devote approximately one fourth of 1 percent of our GNP to such purposes. That is one 400th part. We aren't exactly bankrupting ourselves helping to feed the rest of the world.

A friend has calculated that if the Wise Men from the East had brought the infant Jesus in Bethlehem as a gift a sum equal to the U.S. defense budget he could have given away $150,000 a day, every day of every year from his birth until now, and there would still be money left. We will not feel so hollow if we will bring our behavior toward the poor more in line with our sentiments and sermons.

We choose impotence and then despise ourselves for being impotent. We say that we care and wring our hands, but we do not reduce our consumption of goods or the energy required to produce them.

Because we have a conscience, we become angry and defensive when the plight of our brothers and sisters is called to our attention. We plead helplessness, but none of us is without power to make at least a little difference in the world.

How recover from leanness of the soul? Maybe by becoming leaner of body. Maybe by altering our life-style, using the difference to provide food and the means of growing it for someone who is going to starve if we don't. Maybe by speaking out concerning the nation's priorities, even at the risk of offending our friends. Maybe by encouraging those who hold public trust to use their influence and votes to reflect more accurately the Judeo-Christian faith we claim.

3

How Much Is Enough?

Over Thanksgiving holidays our granddaughters, eleven and seven, presented their Christmas-wants lists. In fact, Laura, the younger, issued three separate editions of hers, each longer than the one before.

There was nothing outrageous or perversely selfish about either's wants. They seemed appropriate enough, and both girls explained that these were merely suggestions from which we could choose. However, the inference was plain that they hoped their gifts would come from the lists. The impact of the culture's values upon those little girls' minds may not be ignored.

Carole, eleven, is into clothes, but not just any skirt or pair of jeans. They should be certain name-brand skirts or jeans. As a seven-year-old, Laura loves dolls, but mainly a particular brand of doll. The world has more serious problems than whether my grandchildren get what they want for Christmas, but their wants—and on a significantly larger scale, ours—connect to the root problem. That problem is our inability to distinguish between want and need. We want so much more than we need and lack the insight or will to discriminate between the two.

A friend writes to his congregation: "How much is enough? When I have more than enough, who suffers? Do I? My children? Those who have less than enough? Is there any connection between my more than enough and their less than enough?"

Such questions haunt the conscience not desensitized by the culture's most common and destructive affliction—greed. How much is enough? Henry Ford, who, if anybody ever did should have had enough, is reported to have answered that question, "Always a little more than you've got." I think he was dialing his own number—and ours. Always a little more—and a little more—no matter how much you already possess.

If you know anything about Jesus' attitudes and values, you will not be surprised that he viewed greed as a subtle and extremely dangerous enemy of the good life. "Beware! Be on your guard against greed of every kind," he once warned, "for even when a man has more than enough, his wealth does not give him life" (Luke 12:15, NEB).

To illustrate the point Jesus told his now-familiar story of a rich man and a beggar named Lazarus. Lazarus lay at the rich man's door, subsisting on the crumbs which fell from the rich man's table. The rich man did not drive the beggar away; neither did he help him. He simply let him be. Indeed, the beggar served a useful social function for the rich man. He took care of the rich man's leftovers.

Both died and in eternity found an unbridgeable chasm separating them, the beggar with God and the rich man in torment. The point of the story is painfully plain. The rich man's affluence had anesthetized his sense of obligation toward the Lazaruses of this world, and it had cost him his soul.

Carlyle Marney, whose legacy will loom even larger as we get farther away from the pain of losing him, called for "an ethic of parsimony," which he defined as "the least that will really do!" How much do we really need to do everything that we really need to do? Aim at that and see how much is left over for our brothers and sisters who have less than they need.

"Not frugality," Marney argued in a lecture at Duke University, "which is a venal sin and crime against nature; not penuriousness, which is a spiritual condition; but parsimony, an empirical, administrative, judgmental principle operative with the least that will really fulfill the end of Creation." I must confess that my wants are far from parsimonious. My needs are somewhat more manageable.

When Albert Einstein, refugee from Hitler's racial insanity, fled to America and became a member of the faculty at Princeton, he was asked to set his own salary. He hesitated, then said he preferred a checking account. At the end of a year, trustees found the great man and his wife had used $1,700!

At Christmas this year I must ask myself, "How can I live more simply that others may simply live?" If I am unwilling to wrestle with that question, how can I pretend to celebrate the birth of Him who had no place to lay his head?

I must not permit myself the easy way out by saying that there is nothing I can do. Recently we were told that if every American driver drove his car three miles less a day the loss of Iranian oil would be fully compensated. That seems ridiculously simple. Surely there are ways of simplifying my life-style, consuming less, getting my "wanter" under control, so that others may have what they need.

4

On Learning How to Give

One night at dinner I sat beside a quiet, unassuming woman who recently provided substantial gifts to the scholarship fund of the university where I work. Nothing in her demeanor suggested that she expected special recognition or thought that she should be entitled to tell the administration how to run the university. Her conversation was warm and genuine, her manner neither detached nor patronizing.

Afterwards I got to thinking about other people I know who have this same rare ability to give with openhanded grace. Why is it that some people appear to enjoy giving without expectation of reward, while others seem to feel that their gift diminishes them unless they are fully compensated in some way?

I decided that giving—true giving—is an exhilarating experience that many of us are afraid to risk having. We are so leery of being duped and manipulated that we never allow ourselves freedom to give without calculation.

Yet, giving is at the heart of our biblical faith. "God so loved that he gave," says one of the most familiar verses of Scripture. "It is more blessed to give than to receive," is another.

I once preached a sermon on that latter verse and a friend who heard the sermon remarked, "It may be blessed to give, but it's more fun to receive." I was glad he had listened long enough to hear the text, but he hadn't heard the sermon. Or at least the sermon hadn't convinced him. He still thought it was all "church-talk."

Of course, if that is so, then Jesus was all wrong. He had an open, not a closed, stance toward life. He reached out with open hands, not with clenched fists. Look at him wherever you see him in the Gospels and you will find him giving—time to teach, strength to heal, privacy to public claims, and on occasion his reputation to outcasts who found dignity and acceptance in his company.

Two of his followers in the early days after his death and resurrection had occasion to practice what he had preached. Peter and John, on the way to the Temple for prayer, were accosted by a crippled beggar asking alms. "Silver and gold have I none," said one, "but such as I have give I thee. . . . Rise up and walk" (Acts 3:6, KJV). Their act contains the elements of a true gift. They gave without making the recipient more dependent. On the contrary, their gift liberated him, enabled him.

I don't want to make this sound like some complicated exercise in spiritual gymnastics, but I think that there are at least five conditions essential to an act of true giving.

One is that it not be partronizing. If I give with the attitude that I am superior, more righteous, harder working and more deserving, or more intelligent than the receiver, I spoil the gift. If in any way my gift robs the recipient of his personhood, makes him feel bad about himself, and renders him less able to take care of himself, I have not ministered to his needs.

A second condition of giving is that it not be obligating. Giving can be a more or less subtle form of control. It can be a way of putting pressure on the receiver. "Look what I did for you. Now how do you intend to show your gratitude?"

A third condition for authentic giving is that it not be crippling to the recipient. Some giving is not only soft-hearted, but soft-headed. The thing that impresses one about the gift of Peter and John to the crippled beggar is that they did not leave him a cripple. They could have flipped him a coin and gone about their business—if they had had a coin to flip. But they did something infinitely more important. They removed his need to beg.

It is easy to stand on the sidelines and take cheap shots at the fiasco of this nation's welfare system or the mess in the financial affairs of our large cities. But the facts seem indisputable that we have created a welfare monster in this country which serves nobody well. It often works hardships on the very persons it purports to help and, what is infinitely worse, it has crippled the will to be self-reliant of hundreds of thousands of our population. Giving is not giving which fails to make the object of our gift better able to cope.

A fourth condition for giving is that it not be self-serving. There is no way to separate out all the mixture of motives in any act. "I don't know why I did it," may be more than an excuse. We don't fully understand ourselves. But we ought to look at why we give. Are we trying to deal with our guilt about what we have done or left undone? Are we giving out of pride? Is it the desire for recognition that makes us give?

Sometimes people use their generosity as a mask for the craving for power. Suppose a person is the largest contributor to his church, but also demands the right to dictate church policy. Is he to be commended for his giving? I think not. He has not given; he has invested in getting his own way. Chances are that when the church stops giving him his way he will cut off his contribution as a poor investment.

The fifth condition is that it not be costless. We give only when what we have left for ourselves is diminished by the act of our giving. Pious assurances that the Lord never lets us make a sacrifice, that he always gives us back more than we give away, cheapens the concept of sacrificial living.

Once King David wanted to set up an altar of sacrifice for the Lord at a certain place. The owner of the property offered to donate the ground to the king. No, said David, he would buy it: "I will not give to the Lord that which costs me nothing" (see 2 Sam. 24:24).

It was a fine sentiment, and right to the heart of the matter. We truly give only when our giving costs us something.

V
O Come, Emmanuel

1

Marion, singing to herself a twelfth-century plain song, is having trouble with the words, and I am trying to help her remember, "O come, O come, Emmanuel,/And ransom captive Israel,/That mourns in lonely exile here,/Until the Son of God appear./Rejoice! Rejoice! Emmanuel Shall come to thee, O Israel!"

The song voices a boundless, timeless hope. Its remembrance is of Israel's captivity in Babylon and the approaching day of the Lord's deliverance. O come, Emmanuel, which name means "God is with us." We Israel—God's people—see with eye of faith the coming of the Deliverer. O come, God-With-Us!

In the Christian calendar the song is most appropriate now, for this is Advent, the beginning of the Christian year and the time to prepare for the special celebration of the Christ child's coming into the world. Advent is an attitude, a stance of faith, whose mood is a complex mixture of anticipation, apprehension, and affirmation.

Anticipation belongs to the spirit of Advent. God's people stand on the tiptoes of expectant hope. "It is time, fully time," Advent signals, "the day of the Lord is at hand." Into our world of incredible mendacity and madness, darkness and despair, the Light shines. God comes to us as a child, embodiment of newness and hope. Let the heart's place be readied for the divine visitation.

Proclamations of his coming know no limitation of time or people, but are our common heritage:

> To us a child is born,
>   to us a son is given;

> and the government will be upon his shoulder,
> and his name will be called
> "Wonderful Counselor, Mighty God,
> Everlasting Father, Prince of Peace" (Isa. 9:6).

Come, Prince of Peace!

The promise is not yet fully realized, but we embrace it, especially at Advent.

> The wolf shall dwell with the lamb,
> and the leopard shall lie down with the kid, . . .
> and a little child shall lead them. . . .
> They shall not hurt or destroy
> in all my holy mountain;
> for the earth shall be full of the knowledge of the Lord
> as the waters cover the sea (Isa. 11:6,9).

The lamb and the kid are not safe with the wolf and the leopard in this kind of world. Hurting and destruction are still too commonplace. The Child has not yet converted our jungle-world into a peaceable kingdom. But at Advent we Christians say with our biblical forefathers, the prophets,

> The glory of the Lord shall be revealed,
> and all flesh shall see it together,
> for the mouth of the Lord has spoken (Isa. 40:5).

If God says so, so be it.

But Advent is more than anticipation. It is also apprehension. We presume when we glibly announce the coming of Emmanuel as occasion for untempered joy. "Woe to you who desire the day of the Lord!" the prophet Amos shouted in the midst of holy services at Bethel seven hundred years ago.

> Why would you have the day of the Lord?
> It is darkness, and not light (5:18).

He comes not only to bless but to judge; he comes not only to establish but to overthrow. In the beautiful Lukan narrative of Christ's birth an aged priest named Simeon comes to Mary and lifts the Holy Child from his mother's arms to bless him and say:

> Behold, this child is set for the fall
> and rising of many in Israel,
> and for a sign that is spoken against
> (and a sword will pierce through
> your own soul also.) (Luke 2:34-35).

The shadow of the cross fell even over the brightness of his birth.

He is more than "gentle Jesus meek and mild." His coming brings divine judgment upon our values and priorities, upon our selfishness, upon our pretense, upon our self-righteous exclusiveness and indifferent inclusiveness. In Advent there is a note of apprehension.

But there is more to Advent than anticipation and apprehension. There is also affirmation. God has acted, and the face of reality is seen in new light. God does not merely encourage us with promises for the future. He has already come, stepping decisively upon the shoreline of our humanity. "When the time had fully come, God sent forth his Son, born of woman, born under the law" (Gal. 4:4) is the way Paul put it.

Elizabeth Barrett Browning wrote to her beloved husband, Robert, "The face of all the world is changed, I think, since first I heard the footsteps of thy soul." So we say of the earth-changing, time-splitting coming of the Lord at Bethlehem. Advent is affirmation that God was in Christ reconciling the world unto himself. From God's side the war is over, but we his people will not yet put down our arms. Above all else the message of Advent is the announcement: "Be reconciled to God."

2

God Came to Live with Us

What moves you to the deepest wonder about the Christmas story? Is it Luke's enchanting narrative of a pure maiden delivering her Child in a stable attended by simple shepherds and heralded by an angelic choir? Or is it Matthew's report of ruthless Herod's stormtroopers butchering Bethlehem's babies in the futile effort to stop Messiah's work before it could begin?

I must tell you that as much as I am moved to awe by these reports, neither so powerfully grips me as does John's picture of Christ painted on a cosmic canvas. John does not begin in the days of Herod the King, but in eternity. As Genesis does, he retreats in time and space to a point where there was only God, nothing else—nothing save God and "The Word." John writes: "In the beginning was the Word, and the Word was with God, and the Word was God" (John 1:1). The identity of the Word is coming clear in John's thought. Jesus is with God and he is God. Moreover, he is the agent of creation. "All things were made through him" (v. 3).

That's fine, we might be saying to ourselves, but what has that to do with Christmas? John answers that by reserving the most startling announcement for last: "The Word was made flesh and dwelt among us, (and we beheld his glory, the glory as of the only begotten of the Father")" (v. 14, KJV). Remember who the Word is. He is God and with God, the means through whom the created universe came to be. The absolutely stunning claim is that such a Personage became human and came to live with us.

To appreciate the impact of John's announcement we need to know that when he wrote there was a group called Gnostics who argued that "flesh" is a vile and filthy thing. Some who held to this view claimed also to be Christians. They could not countenance the idea that Jesus Christ was a real human being. They said that he only seemed to be human. He was really a spirit masquerading as a human. In John's view, such an interpretation destroys the gospel. No, he said, as unbelievable as you may think it, God came as the eternal Word and took up residence in a specific time and place, and he was known by the name of Jesus of Nazareth.

He came to live here, he who was "very God of very God," as one of the Christian creeds defines him. Moreover, he lived not as a potentate in a palace surrounded by all the lavish self-indulgences of man's creativity but as a peasant. Born to poor people, he lived among the poor, shared their lot, and knew their disfranchisement. He who was present when the morning stars first sang together in praise of their Creator identified himself with the meek and humble of the earth. I am awestruck. Most of us are forever trying to figure out how to climb the ladder of prestige, power, and position. He intentionally descended it. And he deliberately stayed.

Dr. Harold C. Warlick, whom I first knew as a defensive back on Furman University's football team and who is now on the faculty of Harvard Divinity School, has a new book entitled *Conquering Loneliness* (Waco: Word Books, 1979, pp. 11-12). In the Introduction he describes his involvement in an urban studies program which took him to the streets of San Francisco. One day he and some other ministers were instructed to put on old clothes and worn-out shoes and get into the line for free lunch at Saint Anthony's Dining Room where 1,300 poor street people are fed daily.

Warlick describes the experience of moving along the line, exchanging nods with others who shared for real the life he had temporarily assumed. He noticed the ways in which they responded to each other, listened to the stories they told, and watched as elderly people scraped leftovers from others' plates into little plastic bags to have something for supper.

"Then," Hal Warlick writes, "as suddenly as the experience had begun for me, it was ended. We got up from the table and made our way back . . . to the streets. I pulled off my dirty, ragged clothes and rejoined the other Baptist ministers from Texas who had been involved in the same experience."

The meaning of the Christmas Event is most sharply defined just at that point. I do not discredit the ministers for changing out of their dirty clothes and resuming their middle-class life. Most of us wouldn't deign to dress up (or down) and get in line for Saint Anthony's free lunch even one time. But the point of Christmas is that God came as Jesus Christ, "born of flesh, born under the law," as Paul put it, and *he stayed*.

The rest of the gospel is that he has promised to stay always. That same John who announced Jesus' cosmic entry into our humanity declares that shortly before the Romans executed the master he told his followers: "I will never leave you alone. I will come to you as the

Holy Spirit and be with you forever" (John 14:18, author's translation). If that is true, why are we so afraid?

3

Waiting for the Vision

God's prophets held up visions of the future before the eyes of his people. "See what great things he has planned!" they said. One vision which made the pulse beat faster is the promise of world peace. Some far-off day nations "shall beat their swords into plowshares and their spears into pruning hooks." Aggression shall cease, and the art of war no longer be taught, because such methods of settling international problems and providing security for all will be seen as obsolete and irrelevant. Like bleeding a patient to cure his sickness, war will one day be a relic of humankind's primitive past.

That day seems now remote, but if we are people of faith, believing the Bible as we say we do, what are we to do with the vision? Does not God call us to be people who are committed to his vision? Anwar Sadat, a Muslim, was recently quoted as saying, "Peace in the Middle East is unavoidable." Must we not also say as Christians and Jews, "If the human race is to survive, peace in the whole world is unavoidable?"

Even at Christmas peace is not a popular word. Indeed, some think it is a subversive word. If it is, God is subversive. It is we, his people in rebellion against our rightful Lord, who speak of the necessity of renewing the arms race and of being prepared to destroy our enemies. We speak of more swords and spears. God speaks of turning what we already have into plowshares and pruning hooks.

The metaphors of plowshares and pruning hooks are a poet's plain way of talking about the path of peace being along the way of food and clothing for all the human family. The specter of world hunger is the world's greatest danger. If the energy and resources being devoted to instruments of destruction were turned into the production of goods to alleviate human suffering, perhaps the vision might begin to take on reality.

We have trouble with visions, in part because we cannot imagine that God's plan for the human race is other than what we plan and work for. Our vision for the world somehow or other always takes the shape of ourselves, and that may not be God's intention at all. It is perilously easy to confuse what we think we want with what God purposes.

What this means is that if we are to be faithful to the vision which God has given through his prophets we shall have to turn our lives around and go in his direction. Such turning around is what the Bible means by repentance. Repentance is not easy for the very reason that it means changing directions, perhaps changing our vision of reality.

We can only glimpse outlines and dim shadows of the future awaiting us perhaps no more than two decades hence. If we can talk about space stations and colonization of the planets without feeling absurd, why is it absurd to talk about world peace?

We have trouble with visions, too, because we are impatient. We demand instant gratification. We cannot wait. But waiting is a holy endeavor. Wrote one of the prophets: "The vision has its own appointed hour; it ripens, it will flower; if it be long, then wait, for it is sure, and it will not be late" (Hab. 2:3, author's translation).

God has his own timetable, and it is not necessarily ours. No cajoling will hasten it or put it off; no delusion or self-deception will alter it. "I know the plans I have for you," says God through another of the prophets, "plans to give you a future and a hope."

What then is the relationship between the vision of the future and the present reality? If the vision is to be actualized in God's own good time, and not before and not later, should we bother with it? Does it not simply come relentlessly like time's ever-rolling stream? Yes, it does, but confidence in the vision gives us great encouragement to risk living in the present as though the future were here. Some day the kingdom of God will fully come. Should not those committed to it begin to live in it now? Would I rather risk being out of step with a system that is doomed to die than be in step with the cadence of God's tomorrow? I want to believe that I shall take such risks, but it is very hard to do.

A young man was arrested for preaching the kingdom of God, wrote E. Stanley Jones of India. When the fellow defended himself that he was preaching only what Jesus had preached long ago, the prosecutor argued, "But the Kingdom of God has not come yet." "It has for me," the young man replied.

"Where there is no vision, the people perish" (Prov. 29:18). To be sure. We cannot survive without hopes and dreams. Christmas revives in us the vision of peace, because the Man of peace once walked among us and filled people's hearts with the vision of what life might be if war should cease. "Prince of peace," the prophet had said he would be called. And so he is. We hail him "Prince of peace." Let not the words be a mockery. Let not the vision die.

4

The True Christmas Gift

When have I really given a gift? Only when my gift meets two conditions which, simply put, are neither obvious nor optional. The first is that the gift must be without strings attached, else it is not a gift. The second is that it must not be costless to me the giver. All the rest about giving is commentary.

The other day while reading my Bible for enjoyment I came across an old familiar verse which, in the light of Christmas, took on fresh meaning. In 2 Corinthians Paul urged the Gentile Christians of Corinth to make a love offering for the Jewish Christians of Jerusalem because they were in need. Those Gentile believers over in Corinth, Greece, had no relationship with the Jewish Christians of Jerusalem. They did not even know each other. In fact, many of the Jewish Christians did not approve of Gentiles being in the church. But Paul said, in essence, "Make them a gift, even if they don't like you. They need you. Make them a gift."

Why give a gift to help somebody you don't know and who probably won't even thank you? Because God has given you the supreme gift of love and forgiveness. Here is how Paul put it: "For you know the grace of our Lord Jesus Christ, that though he was rich, yet for your sake he became poor, so that by his poverty you might become rich" (8:9).

Suddenly the words became for me a concise summary of all the Christmas sermons I had ever heard or preached. Remember, he was rich but became poor, not to show off, or to feel better about being rich, or to make us feel obligated to him for helping us, but that by his becoming poor we might become rich. Love, sheer love—love that is willing to give up riches and embrace poverty so that someone who has known only poverty can know what it feels like to be rich!

Christ's gift of himself epitomizes true giving. His was not a bargain struck, a bribe offered, an exchange made, or an investment put aside. His gift of himself was unconditional and unrestricted.

> Ho, every one who thirsts,
>   come to the waters,
> and he who has no money,
>   come, buy and eat!
> Come, buy wine and milk
>   without money and without price (Isa. 55:1).

Plainly, God is saying: "You all come. I know you don't have the money to pay, but come anyway. You won't lose your dignity. You don't have to beg or kiss my hand. I don't require a performance bond. Just come on and get what you need for yourself and your family. It is my pleasure to give it."

Nor is Christ's gift without cost. "Though he was rich, yet for your sake he became poor" (2 Cor. 8:9). Think of it, he became poor for us! He had always been rich. He got up rich in the morning, ate rich, dressed rich, went to work rich, came home rich, went to bed rich. But then he gave all that up and became poor. He who had had everything became one who had no place to lay his head. He knew the anxiety of being poor, the uncertainty with which the poor live all their days, the draining frustration of not having enough to live on with dignity and to satisfy your basic needs. He who had always been accustomed to the fullness of riches experienced the emptiness of poverty.

He hadn't fallen on hard times and lost his wealth. He had given it away. "For your (my) sake he became poor, so that by his poverty you (I) might become rich." I am staggered by thoughts of the dimensions of his gift. I am embarrassed when I remember my own calculating efforts to love and give. You see, I am rich but I have not become poor that someone who is poor might know a little bit about what I have always taken for granted. But I quickly regain control. *Look,* I reason, *don't be so hard on yourself. You are not God. You are human. You know you can't run a business that way, inviting people to buy what they need without money. You know it isn't sensible to impoverish yourself so that some pauper might enjoy once in his life what you have had every day of yours.*

But there is this inner voice which keeps disturbing me. It says, *True, you are not God. Who said you are? Sometimes you act as though you think you are. The power side of God you like. The giving and loving side of God you won't touch. You like to play God when there is glory in it, but when the call comes to give like God you jump back upon your humanity.*

So Christmas comes to me this year as both gift and challenge. He became poor for me. Can I not be a little more like him? Am I not willing to be a little less rich so that some of my poor brothers and sisters may be a little less poor?

5

A Little Child Shall Lead Them

Above the sofa in our family room hangs a highly prized crewel work called "The Peaceable Kingdom." In part it is valued because it was worked in many, many hours of loving labor by our daughter-in-law, Suzanne. And it is also important to us because of the scene it depicts, the vision of Isaiah the prophet 2,700 years ago. God opened a window upon the future for Isaiah and let him peek at the long longed-for day of world reconciliation and peace.

How could he describe what the eyes of his spirit had seen? What is peace? Two mortal enemies coexisting because each is afraid to attack the other? Is peace living in armed camps, in an atmosphere poisoned with dread, paranoid fear, and constant nerve-shattering vigilance? No, that is not peace, but war that has not yet begun, only awaiting somebody to strike the first blow. Is peace where one holds control over others' life resources and destiny? No, that is tyranny.

What is peace? Peace is where there has been some intervention, perhaps divine, which turns enemies into mutually respecting and supportive colleagues. Peace is a condition which delivers both oppressor and oppressed, both hunter and hunted, both victor and victim, from the terrors of violent death and frees them to enter the kingdom of a common life.

If you were the prophet how would you describe such a longed-for state? Hear how he put it:

> The wolf shall dwell with the lamb,
>   and the leopard shall lie down with the kid,
> and the calf and the lion and the fatling together (Isa. 11:6).

Is the prophet some daffy old coot with his head in the clouds and without a realistic bone in his body? Is it practical nonsense to think about and pray for a day when we shall stop killing one another, and one another's children, and begin caring for each other? Is it pure visionary fuzzy-headedness to believe in God, that God is the one Father of all the human family, and that he will never resign himself to accepting an arrangement in which some are exploiters and oppressors, while others are exploited and oppressed? Can that ancient and persistent sickness be the final word which God pronounces upon his human family? Or is it possible in face of the threat of global nuclear catastrophe to cling to Isaiah's vision of "The Peaceable Kingdom"? We must cherish it or become hopeless. If God is God, someday

Isaiah's vision, shared by all God-loving persons on earth, must come to pass. The vision declares,

> They shall not hurt or destroy
> in all my holy mountain (v. 9).

The hurting and destroying must stop. Lord God, hasten that day's coming and make us instruments of Your peace.

A striking aspect of the vision is the oneness of all life on the planet. Nature, now disordered so that the strong prey upon the weak and the jungle law of survival of the fittest prevails, will be reconciled to itself and to humankind. Could this oneness be possible? God has already made possible the conditions for the coming of "The Peaceable Kingdom" in which the wolf dwells with the lamb.

At the heart of what God has done stands the message of Advent—the coming of the child. At the head of the New Order, the kingdom in which enemies have become brothers and sisters is the one whose birth every Christian relives at this time.

Not only is the heart of our faith found beside a manger in Bethlehem bowing in adoration before a child, but it remains true that the spirit of all children is the key to the coming of the kingdom. What makes the child the keeper of this strange menagerie of wolf and lamb, leopard and kid, calf and lion? What power has the child to change the wolf, the leopard, and the lion so that they are no longer predators who rip and tear and destroy? Perhaps it is only his childlike spirit of trust and love. So we look to the child. The vision of the prophet can only become a reality when we truly let the little child lead.

VI
Don't Wait for Agreement

1

Good relationships depend less upon the parties involved agreeing with one another than upon their accepting one another. If that were not true, a lot of marriages would never last very long, a great many friendships would never develop, and most churches would splinter.

As a matter of fact, the reason so many marriages, friendships, and churches are in trouble today is partly because people do not recognize the difference between agreement and acceptance. As far as I know, the only community where no disagreement exists is a cemetery. Wherever there is life there is difference. That is a large part of what makes our being human so wonderful a privilege. Humankind is a choice maker. When we choose this, we choose against that. Why should we insist that those close to us should elect or be compelled to make the same choices we have made?

I submit that much of our anxiety is caused by the neurotic need to have others agree with us. So there are some marriages in which—according to reports about them—there has never been a disagreement. How frightfully limiting, and how incredibly dull! What that really means is that one partner has ceased being a partner and become a flunky who is present only in body.

Have you ever wanted to be friends with someone who made it plain that the only way he/she would have you for a friend is that you never disagree with him/her? That kind of friendship soon becomes an intolerable burden, does it not? There is no acceptance in it. It is a one-way street.

Sometimes pastors are terribly threatened by disagreement. I heard of a pastor who would present a program to his church staff and then

Don't Wait for Agreement / 63

say, "Everybody who agrees with this proposal say, 'Aye.' All who disagree say, 'I resign.' " I suspect that it was said in jest, but there are plenty of situations in which that kind of conformity is required. If the pastor interprets all expressions of disagreement as acts of disloyalty to God and himself (he ought to be able to tell the difference between God and himself, but sometimes appears unable to do so), the church is in bad trouble.

The dynamics of every healthy community include, I am certain, lively disagreement. It is the "loyal opposition," and it is needed to keep us from getting too comfortable with our narrow and marred visions. To presume that others may need us to correct them but that we don't need them to correct us is to assign ourselves an omniscience which belongs only to God.

A verse in the Book of Amos speaks to me powerfully about this. The prophet is illustrating the inevitability of God's judgment upon evil, and he does so by citing a half dozen well-known proverbs. A proverb is a brief, pithy summary of a chunk of human experience.

The first of these maxims used by Amos says:

> Do two walk together
> unless they have made an appointment? (3:3).

If you meet your neighbor for an early morning brisk walk, it will only be by appointment. Oh, you might once in a while run into him or her, but if you walk together every morning or three times a week, or on Mondays, it will be because you have planned to do so, and each has made the necessary arrangement of his/her schedule to see that it happens.

Now, the King James Version reading of this proverb can be misleading. It has the prophet ask, "Can two walk together, except they be agreed?" The problem here is not so much in the translation as in the meaning assigned to the words. "Except they be agreed" meant simply that they had made an appointment. It did not mean, as it has so often been interpreted, "You can't fellowship with somebody with whom you disagree."

I have heard that interpretation in sermons all my life. It made me uncomfortable even before I knew why. It just didn't sound like

Christ. Then, lo and behold, one day I discovered that Amos did not say that at all. He did not even imply that. He would have deplored the notion it suggests. What he said is that people do not find common ground by accident. They work to find it. They make appointments with one another. They know that relationship happens only where there is some kind of continuing commitment to the process of relationship.

I am deeply troubled by what appears to me to be a serious drift in this society away from the principles of "management by appointment" and toward a rigid totalitarian view of "management by agreement." It is the kind of mentality which fixes another with a flinty look and says coldly, "If you don't agree with us, get out." "If you don't like it here, go somewhere else." "America—love it or leave it!" What ever happened to loving America and wanting to make it a more equitable and just nation?

When people get threatened, their willingness to tolerate disagreement narrows. The more we feel insecure, the less we are willing to allow for those who have a different view from our own. Just now the pressure for agreement rather than commitment to mutual acceptance is the prevailing current in the stream of much of American religious and political life. It bodes ill for the health of the body.

2

Are You Willing to Try?

Remember the cartoon about the psychiatrist sitting at his desk and saying to a patient, "I have good news for you, sir. The examination shows that you do not have an inferiority complex. The problem is that you really are inferior." That may be true of some, but the most common cause of our mediocrity is not overtaxing our ability. It is lack of vision, faith, courage, and will.

To be sure, there are incidents in history when people let their

Don't Wait for Agreement / 65

enthusiasm outrace their good judgment. The Children's Crusade of the thirteenth century was such a case. Thousands of children were organized to march across Europe in an attempt to reach Palestine to free the holy places from the Saracens. Most of them died of illness or starvation before they ever left Italy, or else were sold into slavery.

Mankind is capable of that kind of folly. Jesus once observed that those who thoughtlessly plunge headlong into commitment are like a man who sets out to build a tower without counting the cost or a king who starts a war without calculating the risk.

But that is not the most common source of our ordinariness. We lack what it takes to make us try. When we stand before life's final Arbiter, my guess is that the Almighty will not look over our file and say, "Why were you so reckless as to undertake more than you were capable of doing?" Instead, he will ask, "Why were you so afraid of life that you always played it safe, never risked, and never really tried?"

One of the gospel's best known stories of our Lord's work is the record of his feeding the 5,000 on the Galilean hillside. All four Gospels tell the incident, each emphasizing some detail that caught his attention. All make the point that if his followers are willing to commit what they have to the Lord's use, it will be more than enough. We shall never find out, however, unless we are willing to try.

Look at that hillside scene and it will likely speak to your own condition. The first question to be dealt with is the issue of responsibility. Jesus' disciples saw 5,000 hungry people and began to be uneasy because it was near supper time. Like guests who come and sit and sit until mealtime, refusing to take a hint while members of the family eye each other uncertainly, so these people hung around Jesus as he talked on into late afternoon.

"Send them away, Lord," they whispered to him. I understand the urgency of that request, don't you? Why should I have to deal with this? It's not my problem. I have my own worries and burdens. How come these people impose? "Lord, send them away," we join the disciples in pleading.

The second truth that stands out from this scene is suggested by the answer Philip gave to the challenge of Jesus to his disciples to give the people their supper. "Why, Lord, two hundred denarii worth of bread would not be enough to give each one a morsel" (see John 6:7). A denarius was the price of a day's work. Two hundred days' work would not be sufficient.

Philip is the kind of person who never sees anything but the reasons why "it can't be done." His name is legion, particularly in the churches and other helping institutions. He takes it to be his calling to be ready at all times to arise with his bucket of cold water ready to pour it over the struggling flame of others' enthusiasm. He is an expert in obstacles.

"It won't work," is the heart of his liturgy, whether it be about a personal or a corporate proposal. I listen to a counselee's tale of woe. "What are your options?" I ask at the end. He gives me a laundry list. "Which one seems most promising to you?" I ask. "None of them will work," he quickly informs, and then proceeds to show me why. I dare not offer an option. He has already made it perfectly clear that he has made up his mind that he would rather feel sorry for himself than initiate change.

The third truth emerges from Andrew's discouraged report: "Lord, there is a lad here who has five barley loaves and two fish; but what are they among so many?" Like the chorus in the ancient Greek tragedies who came on stage to chant a résumé of the previous action, so Andrew only restates and reinforces Philip's judgment of the impossibility of the task.

Wouldn't it have been great if Andrew had simply left off the last part of his comment about the situation? Don't you wish he had had the faith and courage to say, "Lord, there is a lad here with five loaves and two fishes, but I'll bet you can make that do"?

What is this story saying to us? It is telling us that the solution to the problem of feeding the 5,000 rested not so much upon the ability of the disciples as upon their pliability. They thought it was a question of finances, a business matter, but it was not. It was not a challenge merely to their ingenuity, but to their imagination and faith, to their courage and obedience.

Their inadequacy was not in their resources, it was in themselves. Are we willing to try?

3

Forgiveness Is Strong Medicine

Do you have any idea how many people are grievously wounded by what somebody has done to them? Are you one who has been hurt? Or are you the hurter? Or both hurter and hurt-ee? I see a lot of people who are hurting—hurting badly. Someone mistreated or misunderstood them. Someone betrayed or rejected them. Someone exploited and discarded them.

People come with an anger that can only be called rage. Others come in despair or desperation. Some come to cry, apologizing through tears for losing control. Some come with elaborate excuses for the one who inflicted the hurt. These bother me most. They are too nice for their own health. When they do permit justifiable indignation to surface, it is awesome to see.

I have been listening to stories of human hurt too many years to tell, and the more I see what we do to one another the more I believe in mankind's nearly limitless capacity for sin. And the more I see the more I am persuaded that forgiveness and reconciliation describe the most powerful force any human being ever experiences. It is powerful for both hurter and hurt-ee.

Jesus understood clearly what we only vaguely and tentatively envision. Forgiveness, he said, is God's favorite word. It is his secret weapon to overcome the power of humankind's rebellion. Forgiveness, if accepted, transforms enemies into friends, rebels into sons and daughters, and despisers of God into lovers of God.

The hitch is, of course, that forgiveness is a two-way street. You know that it is in human relationships. You can say to me to your last breath, "I forgive you," but if I do not wish to be forgiven and reconciled there is no forgiveness and no reconciliation. Thus it is with God. But if the hurter will humble him/herself to accept forgiveness offered by the hurt-ee the most potent force in human experience is released in both lives.

Don't accuse me of some gross oversimplification and flip over to the comics or sports pages—not yet anyway. Hear me out. Forgiveness is hard. It is strong medicine, for both forgiver and forgiven.

Jesus once said to a paralytic, "Son, your sins are forgiven" (Mark 2:5). Some people in the crowd were turned off by his words. "Who can forgive sins but God?" (v. 7), they muttered. Knowing what they were thinking, he said: "Which is easier, to say . . . 'Your sins are forgiven,' or to say, 'Rise, take up your pallet and walk'?" (v. 9). We might suppose that the authentic miracle would be cure of the man's paralysis. Not so, said Jesus. Compared with forgiveness (and in this case contingent upon it), healing was easy. The hard part was unleashing the force of forgiveness in the paralytic's life.

Why did Jesus imply that forgiveness is hard? If you have experienced it, you probably know why. He took sin seriously; we are inclined to condone it. Sin desensitizes us, like leprosy destroys the nerve endings of its victims so that they feel no pain when they injure the affected parts of their bodies. Sin domesticates us, so that we lose the power of discrimination and the capacity for indignation.

A biblical scholar once saw some valuable biblical manuscripts being burned as kindling to start fires. He was appalled and did what he could to save the priceless documents. Why get so worked-up over a few yellowed sheets of parchment? Because he was a scholar and was sensitive to the value of those documents.

If you are inclined to take forgiveness lightly, as though to say, "What's the problem?" rest assured that you do not take sin seriously. One of this country's foremost psychotherapists Karl Menninger has written a book entitled, *Whatever Became of Sin?* Good question.

Jesus must have felt that forgiveness is hard, not only because he considered sin a serious matter, but also because of what forgiveness does to the one forgiven. It means admitting that you were wrong and that your wrongdoing is not justifiable, and most of all, your wrongdoing has done grievous hurt to the one from whom you seek forgiveness. Such admissions do not come lightly. The two hardest words in the English language are probably, "Forgive me."

Jesus must have thought that forgiveness is hard for another reason. It is a powerful force in the life of the forgiver. To be willing to forgive is to have a touch of the divine. Nothing heals the hurt heart like forgiveness. Nothing soothes the wounded pride like forgiveness. Nothing melts the icy wall of isolation like forgiveness. Nothing restores broken relationships like forgiveness.

Forgiveness is not "acting as though nothing happened." I think it has been represented as such, but that is wrong. Forgiveness is beginning again, but with a never-before-experienced closeness, with a greatly heightened sense of the preciousness of a trust relationship, and with a new and deeper commitment to nourish what has been restored that it not be broken ever again.

4

Dealing with Rejection

What do you do when you offer the hand of forgiveness and the one you offer it to spits on it? A couple of weeks ago I wrote in this column about the power of forgiveness. I thought I had finished with the subject for the time being, but now I realize that I have not.

A friend responded to the column with a question: "After one forgives and the forgiveness is not accepted—what then?" Hmm. Good question.

What do you do if you are rejected? It happens to everybody, maybe not at the same level to everybody, but it happens. I remember saying in the column that forgiveness is a two-way street, that it may be as hard to receive it as to give it. But I think that my friend's observation is correct. I did not deal with forgiveness rejected.

Maybe I did not deal with it because the fear of rejection is very real to me. Some people seem to have less need for others' approval than I have. Why this is so I am not sure. It is too simple to say that I was made insecure by being orphaned before the age of three. All I know is that I want people to like me. I need it bad.

And that need plagues me as a minister, because I also badly need to feel that God approves of me. The conflict arising out of the need to have God's approval and people's approval is often painful. How be prophetic and still say only what people are pleased to hear?

Jesus, who knew a little about rejection, once asked his contemporaries, "Which of the prophets did your fathers not persecute?" That has disturbing implications. If everybody likes what the preacher preaches, he may need to ask himself some serious questions about his standing with God.

I fantasize about being less wishy-washy about this, and less conflicted over it. Sometimes I resolve to be a prophet and flail away with both fists. But I want to be the Reverend Mr. Nice who hands out candy sticks to the children and sugar sticks from the pulpit. I have done some of both.

Jesus, who strikes me as the most mature personality in history, and who did not seem to be either cowed or soured by rejection, once gave a word which is both warning and consolation: "Beware when all people speak well of you." If he had said, "Beware of wanting all to speak well of you," I could relate to the words even more than I already do.

A good place to begin understanding what Jesus thought about the way to deal with rejection is to read Matthew 10. This passage contains a set of instructions to his disciples as they are sent to preach in the villages of Galilee. One instruction is especially relevant: "and if any one will not receive you or listen to your words, shake off the dust from your feet as you leave that house or town" (Matt. 10:14).

The words conjure up an intriguing scene of the two missionaries standing at the edge of a town that has thrown them out, carefully and vigorously shaking their feet to be sure that they did not carry any residue of the town to their next assignment. Maybe the church should institute a sacrament of shaking the dust off your feet. I know some people who need that service.

Hurt and rejected, these people have done all they could to mend the brokenness, but it takes two to do the mending, and the other will not have it. So the one who has been rejected feels miserable, maybe bitter, or worse, guilty. "Where did I fail," he/she asks?

Jesus would say, "Don't you think it is time to shake the dust off your feet about this? Is it not time to let it go? Have you not hurt enough? Can you give up and accept that the brokenness will never be mended short of some miracle of God? Is it not time to resume your life, accepting as part of its coloring this terrible experience of being rejected?"

But, you may be thinking, I can't do that. I can't give up or quit loving. Besides, didn't the Lord command us to forgive seventy times seven, and to pray without ceasing? Yes, he did, but he also commended the service of foot-shaking when it is called for.

A time comes when you need to say, "Well, that is that. I have grieved and wrung my hands enough; I have cried enough tears and lost enough sleep. I have been depressed long enough, felt guilty long enough, and unwanted long enough. It is time to put that away and begin living again." That is what shaking the dust off your feet is all about.

Does this sound harsh and insensitive to you? I hope not. Believe me, I have been there. I do not want to be a callous person. I am glad that I am vulnerable, that what other people think is important to me. But I must not allow myself forever to be held hostage to grief, whatever its source. Somewhere, sometime, I have to say, "It is time to live again."

And what of the person who spits on your outstretched hand? You have to let that go, too. Spitting back won't help, and hanging around to be a convenient target for the other's continued rejection won't either. There comes a time to shake your feet.

5

On Learning to Forgive Oneself

Twice recently this column was on forgiveness—once about the need to forgive others so that we can live without debilitating bitterness, and the second time about "shaking the dust off one's feet" when faced with an unreconcilable conflict so that one can get beyond the humiliation of being rejected.

I thought I had finished with the matter, but it keeps coming up. A third urgent question has arisen: "How forgive oneself?" I have known people who claimed that they are never bothered by a guilty conscience. I always suspected that they were whistling in the dark, trying to avoid dealing with the pain of moral failure. A few may have been psychopathic, having no conscience. Most of us know firsthand what it is to be ashamed.

Normal people confess with Paul, "I don't do the good I want to do; instead, I do the evil that I do not want to do" (Rom. 7:19, GNB). The issue is not whether healthy-minded persons should suffer remorse, but how to handle remorse when it overwhelms one. How forgive oneself?

Although true, it is too simple to say, "You can't forgive yourself, only God can forgive. Trust him. He forgives those who want forgiveness." Apt as not you have already said that to yourself a thousand times if you are one of those suffering a crushing burden of guilt. But you still carry it.

We have to begin at another question: "Why do I refuse to give up this obsession with my guilt? Why can't I accept God's forgiveness?" As a counselor I commonly hear three answers to that question. First, "I cannot be forgiven because I have been so bad." The flip side of this extreme self-reproach is the second answer. "God has been so good to me, how can I excuse myself for the rotten things I have done?" The third is, "I really love those I have wronged and am so ashamed of what I have done to them that I can never forgive myself."

Those three responses are almost like an automatic reflex. I hear them over and over from people whose lives are miserable because they cannot deal with their guilt. They are honest answers, more's the pity, well-intentioned efforts to express how such people see themselves.

But they are unrealistic and not very helpful. If we are in the condition of being unable to get relief from the burden of guilt, we need to explore some other possibilities. Such exploration will proba-

Don't Wait for Agreement / 73

bly be painful, like lancing a boil or probing for a buried splinter in the end of your finger. Recoiling from the pain of such an experience is only human, but the wound may not heal otherwise.

One possibility that needs exploring is that you and I may be clinging to guilt as a form of self-inflicted punishment. Somehow or other, if I flagellate my spirit long enough and severely enough I may be able to make up to God and to those I have wronged for what I did. If I surrendered my guilt to the Lord and accepted his forgiveness, how would I be able to pay for my wrongdoing? Guilt, then, has become a way of feeling good about feeling bad.

You may be saying right now as you read this, "Well, it sure doesn't feel like I'm feeling good. I'm so miserable I am about to die." Maybe so, but what if the worse you feel the more you also feel, "Well, I'm doing what I ought to be doing. I'm paying for my sins"? In that case, remorse is reinforced as a way of rectifying the wrong you committed. And it will not work. It never works. You sink deeper into the reinforced guilt feelings, and you make more miserable the lives of the very persons you want to make restitution to.

A second possibility one wallowing in guilt and despair needs to explore is this: "Am I insisting that I am a special case?" Am I saying, "Oh yes, I believe that God forgives anyone who wants to be forgiven, but he can't forgive me"? Come now, are you taking yourself too seriously? Paul is my most admired hero, except Jesus, but I wish he had left unsaid some things in his letters. One was to call himself the chief of sinners. I am sure he did not mean to be bragging, but I suspect that there have been a few who outdid him in the sin department.

Maybe you and I take ourselves too seriously when it comes to the Department of Depravity. This is not to suggest that our sins are trifles. It is to say that Gods grace is surely greater than our sins, else he is not God and grace is not grace.

One other question about this ever-present burden of guilt. "Am I too proud to let it go?" Am I too stubborn to ask? Am I one who insists on "paying my own way" even with God? Am I saying, "I got myself into this mess; now by heaven, I'll get myself out"?

The problem is, we really cannot forgive ourselves. Someone else must say the word that releases us from prison; someone else must remove the handcuffs from our wrists. And that is precisely what Christ offers—to set us free.

VII
Baffling Reflections in a Mirror

1

An ancient creation legend tells that at the beginning God invited all the tiny seeds of life to appear before him to say what they wanted to become, "I want to swim in the water," said one, and God made fish with fins and gills. Another said, "I want to fly in the air, soaring above the earth," so God made birds, from the mighty eagle to the tiny swallow.

A third life-seed asked to be made to run upon the ground and roam the forest. Thus God made animals with strong legs. Last came a life-seed which said, "I want to be able to understand, to know what and why things are." And God said, "You have asked for the highest gift," and he made humankind.

The legend is fancy, but truth is often conveyed in story. Humankind is characterized by the need to know the what and why of reality. The measure of our species' difference from other species is the search for understanding. Traveling through the sea like a fish, or soaring in the air like an eagle, or speeding over land faster than a gazelle is not enough for humankind. We are what someone has called "meaning mongers."

The faith of the Bible is related to the issue of meaning. In countless places and ways it says that the meaning of life is found in God's disclosure of himself, that we can never resolve the deep craving within us for understanding until we turn to God. Christians believe that ultimate meaning is found in God's revelation through Jesus Christ. What we mean by this is not that all other religions are spurious, but that who God is, what he has done, and what he intends to do are fully expressed in Christ. This is to say that if we understood him fully we would have the answer to all "what and why."

In such a sense it may be said that "Christ is the answer." We do not mean by that claim that the Christian has all the answers, that all he (she) needs is to have enough faith in Christ and there would be no more mystery. We do not suppose for a moment that we have all the answers. We believe in and trust the Answerer.

The enlightened Christian does not deny that God has given glimpses of meaning in many ways—nature, history, persons whose lives become windows on the street for us—but for Christians the ultimate word is Christ. "In him all the fulness of God was pleased to dwell" (Col. 1:19). We know, but like children who know and trust their parents, we do not fully understand.

Nowhere is this better said than in Paul's timeless ode to love, 1 Corinthians 13. Love, he said, is more to be desired than anything else, including knowledge, for knowledge is always partial and subject to revision. "At present we only see the baffling reflections in a mirror, but then it will be face to face; at present I am learning bit by bit, but then I shall understand, as all along I have myself been understood" (v. 12, Moffatt). Thus the apostle described the quest to know. What we see is always a reflection, imperfect and distorted as a mirror image. I cannot really see myself. The mirror image of me is not the real thing, but a reversal of my appearance—right to left and left to right. So my need to know is forever unsatisfied.

A modern illustration of our human dilemma may be suggested. Life is like a movie being made. The filming appears to an onlooker as a disorganized helter-skelter of confusion. Perhaps, for example, all the scenes involving a certain group of actors and a particular location will be made at one time, although they do not logically occur together. The lines and action of the scenes shot therefore make an appearance of incoherence.

But the director knows what he is doing. He has the whole movie in his mind, and when he gets it all spliced together it will make sense. We Christians may so envision life. God knows what he is about. He is putting the pieces together in ways that we do not comprehend. But when he invites us to the premiere and we see it all unfold on his cosmic screen, and discover our role, minor though it be, we shall understand.

A word of caution. To believe that God is in charge of making the movie called "Life" is not the same as saying that everything that happens is by his instruction and under his direction. That would make God villainous. It is to say that when everything comes together we shall see that the whole cosmic drama has a coherent theme and a proper conclusion. We shall also rejoice that we were invited to participate in the making of the movie.

To pursue the parable, not every scene shot at the director's instruction will be usable. He cannot always guarantee that the actors will follow his directions, or that something may not go awry on the set. The director may make a dozen retakes, and afterwards conclude that the entire sequence is a diversion that needs to be cut out of the film. But when the film is finally put together it will make sense. Trust the Director.

2
Over and Above

When my martyr complex gets going, I can work up a good case of the "self-pities" in a hurry. Overscheduled and underappreciated, that's what I am. I say and write all this profound stuff and some people have the gall to criticize. How dare anybody think I am too liberal or too conservative? The truth is, I am just right, a candidate for canonization.

The best antidote I have found for this chronic condition is to read the Bible and take it seriously, not just sentimentally. Fortunately I have a Bible and I can read, so I do. It usually helps me get myself back into perspective, especially if I read about Jesus and what he said.

An important message that I keep getting from Jesus is that you and I are not extraordinary, that there is not as much difference between us Christians and the rest of our society as we like to pretend. Now, there have been times when being a Christian was dangerous. Somebody might nail you to a cross or throw you into an arena with the lions. Once in a while a Christian was drowned, his tormentors resolving to "baptize" him with a vengeance.

But in my entire life I have never read an account of a Christian in America being put to death because he was a Christian. Or even jailed very often. There is a wonderful verse in 1 Peter 4 which reads, "Yet if one suffers as a Christian, let him not be ashamed, but under that name let him glorify God" (v. 16).

You have to read that either with your tongue in your cheek or treat it as a curious historical reference. You and I haven't suffered as Christians, and aren't about to invite it, either. We do like to play the church game of make-believe suffering for Jesus. It helps us deal with Jesus' call for self-denial. But we are just playing games. We sing, "Jesus, keep me near the cross," but you can bet that a real cross would find few bearers in the church. Another favorite that facilitates our self-deception is that old stand-by, "All to Jesus I surrender." Really? Who among us has heard Jesus say, "Go and sell all you have and give the money to the poor, . . . and come and follow me?" (Matt. 19:21, GNB).

When our son was a little boy on Marshall Terrace in Danville, Virginia, he had a hard time keeping up with the other kids because he was born with a serious heart defect that made it impossible for him to run fast or far. The street was full of kids all summer and on nonschool days, and many a time I have looked out and seen the great American kid game of cops and robbers or cowboys and Indians or charging army taking place in the street and Roland would be about ten yards behind, calling out, "Come on, men, follow me!" That is too often the voice and position of the church. We talk as though we are leading the world when in fact we are trailing along about ten yards behind.

If you want a sobering experience, sit down and read the Sermon on the Mount (you find it in Matt. 5—7), asking yourself from time to time, "Did Jesus really mean this, or was he just making up pious words?" If you find my suggestion offensive and disrespectful of the

Lord, do you think our more ordinary way of dealing with them more acceptable? What we do about them most of the time is to read them gravely with our most religious tone of voice, and then assume that because we have spoken the words we have lived by them.

Jesus was so radical that the Roman establishment executed him as a dangerous enemy of the state. What makes us think he would be less a threat to our political/economic/military establishment? He kept talking about values, priorities, causes, and goals. The "trouble" with Jesus was: all of his views and values were so at odds with his own time that people could not take him. It is curious to me, when I allow myself to think about it much, that we have so domesticated Jesus and perfumed his words that he is at home in our parlors and our finest churches.

Read these words in a contemporary translation: "You have heard that it was said, 'Love your friends, hate your enemies.' But now I tell you: love your enemies and pray for those who persecute you, so that you may become sons of your Father in heaven. . . . Why should God reward you if you love only the people who love you? . . . And if you speak only to your friends, have you done anything out of the ordinary?" (Matt. 5:43-47, GNB).

The truth is, I haven't done anything extraordinary. When the Lord says to me, "What more have you done than people who made no pretense of being religious?" I shall have to say to him, "Not much, Lord, not much."

3

Old Wine in New Wineskins

A colleague I like asked if I am still making predictable observations about obvious issues. The jest was about this weekly effort. I confessed that I am trying to manage a grin to conceal the wince.

At the time, I considered the question clever and mostly accurate.

Further reflection (no sleep lost over it) convinces me that it describes me to a tee. I am predictable and I do write about obvious issues. Novelty is not my gift.

No apology for being a stick-in-the-mud, but I question whether the country needs more novelty. Seems to me "we've gone about as far as we can go" in every which way—stimulating, titillating, satiating—until we have gotten down to the bottom of the well where the slime collects. A lot of new stuff smells like garbage, probably because it is garbage.

Indeed, I question that there is much new in either vice or virtue. Both are as predictable as human nature. We belong to a once-a-year club (the best kind to belong to). Every Christmas we get together in somebody's house, each couple bringing a covered dish and two for-fun presents. About ten years ago somebody brought an absurd-looking plaster-of-paris bird. The following Christmas the bird's new owner gilded the thing, wrapped it, and brought it back to the party. Every year since that dratted bird has turned up, repainted and looking new. Now an electrical bird noise has been added. But though wrapped in a different box, it is always the same old bird.

The more I think about it the less I am upset at being predictable. The Bible does not contain too many surprises, but it is still the world's best seller. Besides, God has been saying the same old thing through the centuries, and we still can't seem to get it right.

"Thou shalt have no other gods besides Me," he commands (see Ex. 20). No novelty or ambiguity in that. But idolatry hasn't gone away; it just keeps showing up in a different box.

"Thou shalt not bear false witness," God says. But the big lie and the fast move were never more highly rated.

"Thou shalt not steal," God says. But we have turned that old sin into an art.

Sunday's paper was full of stories of people behaving predictably. There is the ex-Congressman who complains that he was unfairly treated by the FBI because it "entrapped" him to take a bribe. After all, Congressmen should not be tempted to take bribes. They are human, and may not be able to turn down an innocent little swindle of the taxpayers.

Baffling Reflections in a Mirror / 81

Then there was the story of the popular young male star who makes no bones about his bad-conduct discharge from the U. S. Marines, his attempted car theft, and his jail term. Just an all-American type whom your son will model after, or your daughter marry.

Or, if you are not yet sufficiently impressed with the predictability of sin, you may wish to read about the religious conversion experience of one of our modern-day saints, a five-time loser at the marriage altar and now a distinguished Washington lady.

I suspect that at heart we are all fairly predictable. Jesus said so. "By their fruits you shall know them," he said without novelty. "Do people gather grapes from thorns, or figs from thistles?" (see Luke 6:44). he asked with relentless logic. You don't have to be very smart to tell a grapevine from a thornbush.

People do not characteristically behave simply on impulse. Rather, they act out what is inside them. As Father John Powell argues persuasively, our behavior is shaped by the vision we carry within our minds as to the nature of ourselves, others, God, and the world. If you would change your life, change your vision. People with an unaltered vision will, with rare exception, behave predictably. Change the machinery and you change the product.

If we appear to be unpredictable, it is often that we are issuing false bulletins to ourselves and others as to what we are up to. Just possibly we are on occasion "acting out of character." More likely we are behaving in character, and a straight line of predictability can be drawn through most of our unguarded behaviors. The wolf may dress in sheep's clothing and baa like a lamb, but he still devours the sheep.

But predictability is not banality or triteness. It is not consistency which condemns the writing hack to mediocrity. It could be lack of talent. Or effort. If one may be pardoned for paraphrasing the Master phrasemaker, Jesus, perhaps we should work harder at putting the old wine into new wineskins. Just don't be fooled by the wineskins.

4

Look At Me

Remember the fable of the turtle who came up with the clever plan to fly? He persuaded the eagle to grasp a stick in his claws, the turtle took hold with his beak, and away they went soaring above the hills. All was going splendidly until one of the animals below looked up at the remarkable sight and exclaimed, "What a clever idea! Who ever thought of that?" The turtle, unable to restrain his pride, shouted down, "I did!" and plummeted to his death.

Fables are about foibles of people, of course, and the inordinate desire for recognition is the undoing of us all. A friend has this pithy saying on a plaque behind his desk: "There is no limit to what a man can accomplish if he doesn't care who gets the credit."

I doubt that there is a more severe test of one's character than at the point of "Who gets the credit?" Like the turtle, we find it impossible to stick to the assignment. We simply have to open our mouths to be sure that everybody knows how smart we are.

In a certain church after Sunday-morning worship the preacher's little boy climbed up on a chair behind the pulpit and shouted into the microphone as the people were filing out, "Look at me, I'm up in the pulpit!" One long-suffering parishioner was heard to mutter aloud, "My, my, how many times I have heard that sermon!"

The "look-at-me" sermon is not confined to the pulpit. One has the feeling that it can be heard almost anywhere. The need that produces it may be seen at work in legislative halls, judges' chambers, presidential suites, or the humblest home. The "look-at-me" character flaw destroys relationships. It may even cause a man with great power to do massive harm to a nation or the world.

The root problem of human pride has been with us for some time. That, indeed, is the meaning of the Genesis story of the fall of man in the Garden of Eden. When the serpent promised Adam and Eve that they would "be as gods," he was tickling the most susceptible place in the human psyche. We all want to be gods, to stand astride our own little world, issue edicts and exercise mastery over all that comes and goes.

The "look-at-me" syndrome evidences a neurotic fear of not having control. We suspect that we are powerless. We are anxiety driven because we cannot trust the life-process to let us occupy the place we ought to have, so we must force events and noisily push ourselves on others with unseemly or coercive behavior.

Whoever takes Jesus as model must be impressed that his life was a direct contradiction of the "look-at-me" style. He characteristically called himself "servant." "I did not come to be served," he said, "but to serve." "He who is greatest among you shall be servant of all," he told his disciples.

Examples of his servant model in the Gospels are well-nigh inexhaustible. Read, for instance, the account in John 13 of his washing his disciples' feet. John introduces this act of plain and humble service with a remarkable theological statement. He says that Jesus, knowing who he was and where he had come from (God), and where he was going (to God), rose from supper, laid aside his robe, girded himself with a towel, took a basin of water and began without announcement to wash his disciples' feet.

The suggestion is inescapable that Jesus' absolute certainty about his own identity made it possible for him to perform the act of a slave. He did not preface the act with an explanation that although he was really far above such menial service, yet to set an example he would perform it. He felt no prideful need to say, "Look-at-me."

No community can get along without the volunteer services of many citizens. All who engage in such service do so for a reason—probably a variety of reasons. In part, we may be dealing with our need for recognition; in part, with our guilt because we have more than others of this world's goods; in part, because we really care about people. Whatever be the reasons, a man or woman needs to recognize in himself the human tendency to interpret the worth of what he does in terms of the recognition he gets for doing it.

Sir Thomas More, hero and martyr of Henry the Eighth's England, once wrote to his children's tutor: "The more I see the difficulty of getting rid of this pest of pride the more do I see the necessity of setting to work at it from childhood.... That this plague of vainglory may be banished far from my children, I do desire that you and their mother and all their friends would sing this song to them, and repeat it, and beat it into their heads, that vainglory is a thing despicable, and to be spit upon; and that there is nothing more sublime than that humble modesty so often praised by Christ."

VIII
Life's Unexpected Dividends

1

Long before I ever heard of serendipity I had experienced it. If somebody had asked me when I was growing up out in Oklahoma if I had had any serendipity lately I probably would have answered, "My grandma won't even let us boys drink coffee, much less—what did you say that was?"

After learning about serendipity I still suspected that it was one of those cutesy coined words found in popular self-help literature designed to make a fast buck by making shallow readers feel better about being shallow. Imagine my surprise to find serendipity right there under the "S-es" in my 1934 edition of *Webster's New International Unabridged Dictionary.*

"Serendipity: The gift of finding valuable or agreeable things not sought for." Horace Walpole, no less, coined the word in the eighteenth century. He had a tale about three "Princes of Serendip" who in their travels were always discovering, by chance or by sagacity, things they did not seek.

We all do, provided our senses are alerted to catch the signals. My favorite missionary, Paul, was forever experiencing serendipity. Somebody would beat up on him, throw him in jail, or otherwise try to shut him up or do him in, and the next thing he knew some new opportunity, some new and unexpected bonus would present itself. They jailed him in Philippi and he got to preach to the jailer and the prisoners. They laughed him out of Athens and he opened a great work in Corinth. They mobbed him in Jerusalem and he wound up getting to go to Rome.

One of his best-loved letters is Philippians. He felt especially close to that congregation, for they were always sending him financial help and expressing their love for him. He writes to them from prison. Prison is no picnic or vacation. It could be the end of him if he were found guilty of the false charges against him. Rarely have jails been much fun for the prisoner. Evidently the one Paul was occupying when he wrote Philippians was no exception. He knew that the people to whom he was writing had been worried about him, too. What would happen to him? No doubt there were severe hardships. But, guess what? There were also gifts—serendipities.

"I am glad to tell you, brothers, that the things that happened to me have actually been a help to the Good News," he wrote. How in the world could that be? Read on: "My chains, in Christ, have become famous not only all over the Praetorium but everywhere" (Phil. 1:12-13, *The Jerusalem Bible*). People were talking about this prisoner and discussing his case—the fact that he was in jail because of his devotion to One called Christ—all around the military establishment. In the barracks, on the parade ground, in the cells, wherever people got together to exchange news about the day's happenings. Christ was getting known in a manner Paul would never have been able to accomplish as a free man.

But there is more. "And most of the brothers have taken courage in the Lord from these chains of mine and are getting more and more daring in announcing the Message without any fear" (v. 14, *The Jerusalem Bible*). Another unexpected dividend. Jailing the most effective spokesman the church had to the Gentile world had not silenced the voice of the good news. It had only served to multiply it. Some of the brothers who had previously been a bit cautious in their witnessing to Christ were now becoming courageous. If Paul could go to jail for his witness to Christ, they also must dare to speak with greater boldness.

Indeed, there was a most curious aspect of this second serendipity. "Some . . . are doing it just out of rivalry and competition (and) do not mind if they make my chains heavier to bear. But does it matter? Whether from dishonest motives or in sincerity, Christ is proclaimed; and that makes me happy" (vv. 15-18, *The Jerusalem Bible*). Hard as it was for Paul to live with, some of his fellow Christians did not think he was just dandy. They were glad to see him get his lumps. It did not matter. More important than whether these people preached Christ out of love or jealousy toward Paul, the important thing was that the gospel was being preached as never before. God has hit many a straight lick with a crooked stick, hasn't he? He uses you and me, doesn't he?

There is one more serendipity. "I know that through your prayers and the help of the Spirit of Jesus Christ this will turn out for my deliverance" (v. 19, *The Jerusalem Bible*). People who love Paul, people such as the Philippians, are really praying for him now that his life is imperiled, as never before. His critical situation has upped the voltage of their prayerful concern on his behalf. With that kind of outpouring of human love and with the constant help of the Spirit, how could it be other than all right?

Life has, to use Walpole's words, "valuable or agreeable things not sought for." There is another way of putting it. Every situation, no matter how desperate, has a "redemptive dimension." God can teach us something or do something for us, in the worst prison that he may not ever be able to do for us without it. You don't seek it, but you do not ignore it, either.

2

The Nature and Uses of Prayer

For a lot of years we have known each other. So I figured she meant business when she came up and said, "I need to come and talk with you about prayer." Some of the history behind that need I know about, including critical illness in the family. People who believe much in God sooner or later are going to have to deal with the issue, "Does it do any good to pray?"

The nature and uses of prayer are as many-splendored as the occasions of our lives. When his disciples asked Jesus to teach them to pray (in response to the example of prayer life they witnessed in him) he gave them a simple but profound model. We call it the Lord's Prayer. When next you repeat the Lord's Prayer notice that it has two distinct parts. First, there are petitions about God and his work. I like to call these the "Thou-petitions." "Thy Name be reverenced, Thy Kingdom come, Thy will be done" (author's translation).

People who suppose that God runs his business without the aid or interest of his people, and that God's shop stays open twenty-four hours a day, 365 days a year, whether we pay any attention or not, need to take note of Jesus' prayer. Why pray that God's name—his character and nature—be hallowed, that his kingdom come and his will be done, unless our praying makes some difference in that cosmic plan?

Surely Jesus was not giving the prayer as a kind of pious exercise which may make the one who prays feel better but which has no other value? I hardly think so. I believe that he is saying to us that we are dynamically engaged with God in the divine intention to make this world his kingdom.

Notice that the second half of the prayer is also composed of petitions, these being "We-petitions." "Give us our food for today, forgive our debts as we forgive our debtors, and do not let us fall into temptation" (author's translation).

Prayer, then, is not merely a "gimme" self-indulgence for those too weak or trifling to wade into the deep water and swim for themselves. It is a daring response to the invitation of the Lord of all Being to participate with him in the making of the world and the making of ourselves.

Sometimes prayer is an argument, or a protest. For me at least, prayer is not infrequently in the form of a question. Why, God? There is abundant precedent for that. Job argued with God, questioned his judgment and even his character. Moses argued with God. "Why did you bring me out here into this desert with all these complaining Israelites?" Even Jesus questioned his Father. "Why have you forsaken me?" he asked in desperation from the cross.

I find that much of my praying is the nonverbal enjoyment of contemplation, thinking about God, trying to understand what he is up to, how I fit into his purpose, and what my relationship with him and the world is. I read the Bible a lot, which to me is an important kind of praying, for then I feel I am perhaps most open and receptive to what God is trying to get me to hear.

People who know and care for each other do not have to be talking all the time to communicate. Silence is at least as important and healing as sound. He speaks to me in the silence. I am glad to be with God when I don't want anything from him except to know his Presence.

But there are other times when I want with a deep, immeasurable need. These are times when I am afraid, or depressed, or empty, or terribly alone, or full of grief. Sometimes I am just plain tired. Sometimes I am embarrassed about some shoddy piece of behavior, some hurtful word or act. Then I want more than a Cosmic Listener, more than a Righteous Observer, more than an Absentee Landlord. I want a Father.

Jesus addressed God as "Abba," the nearest English equivalent to which is "Daddy," or even "Papa." I am not too grown up and too self-assured to need a Papa. Not all the time, you know, but when I need him I really need him.

Moreover, the Lord's Prayer suggests that God needs my efforts, too. Once I would have denied that, supposing that for God to need me means that he is not all-powerful and therefore not really God. But I am to pray and work toward the divine intention that his Kingdom come and his will be done in earth.

I am a daddy, and much of the meaning of my life derives from being called by certain very important people, "Daddy," or "Pop." My children are long since grown and have children of their own. But they still need their daddy once in a while, and I am blessed by being that to them.

They are also my colleagues and equals, capable of helping me as I can sometimes help them. Our relationship is infinitely richer than if they said, "Now we are grown. We don't need you anymore as children need a father. So, you do your thing and we'll do ours. Once in a while we shall check with you to see how you are and let you know how it is with us." There is more to family than that one-dimensional view suggests.

Prayer is not a substitute for your own efforts. Neither is it a last-ditch cry of desperation. It is a sharing of yourself with God, making yourself available both to receive and give help.

3

Does Religion Really Matter?

When life gets hard and you have a tough time deciding what is right, where does your religion come in? Does it help you draw "the bottom line" in matters that matter? When it comes to the problem of energy, or inflation, or the hostages, or the Russians, or who will be elected President, does it even occur to us to ask, "What is God's will?" Or is his authority confined to issues of personal behavior and the correct way to worship him?

A sentence from Edward Gibbon's famous six-volume *The Decline and Fall of the Roman Empire* is painfully appropriate to the current American scene: "The various modes of worship which prevailed in the Roman world were all considered by the people as equally true, by the philosophers as equally false, and by the magistrates as equally useful." To the degree that that was true, religion made no difference at all.

Gibbon, whose first volume of *Decline and Fall* appeared just four months before the outbreak of the American Revolution, had little use for religion. Being a thorough-going rationalist, he saw religion, and especially Christianity, as a weakening influence on Rome's earlier aggressive policy which brought her to the zenith of power.

Gibbon's historical accuracy has long been suspect for several reasons, but his judgment about religion in the Roman Empire bears thoughtful examination in the light of late twentieth-century America. Religion has rarely been more popular and enjoyed greater visibility. But the quality of American religion and the influence it has upon policies and priorities are quite another matter.

Is it true, as Gibbon said it was in Rome, that here "the various modes of worship . . . [are] considered by the people as equally true?" The evidence that that is the case is hard to deny. All you need to do is look at the "Religion" section of the weekend newspaper, turn on the radio or TV, or listen to the voice in the street. Of the proliferation of religion there is no end. Got a scheme to make money? Baptize it and call it religion. People will buy the proposition all the more readily if you are flamboyant and self-assured. Americans, like the Athenians of Paul's time, find religion irrestible. Walking through the streets of Athens, Paul noticed statues and altars on every hand. One even announced, "To an Unknown God." Athenians wanted to be certain that no religion was overlooked. Paul said wryly, "I see that you people are very religious."

He could say it here and now, too. Like Gibbon's Romans and Paul's Athenians, we are people who approve of all religions. During half-time at a football game last fall, my wife and I noticed several smiling young women pinning flowers to the lapels of college boys and collecting dollars, occasionally as much as five dollars—whatever the young man would give. The girls represented a notorious cult which owns hundreds of millions of dollars of real estate in this country, and which gets its money by such deceptive methods. Marion went up to a young man who had just handed over $5.00 and asked him if he knew what he had contributed to. He said he didn't but was sure it was for a good cause! That is what comes from living in an environment where all religions are considered equally true.

We are no better off if the second part of Gibbon's claim about Rome is true of us: "The various modes of worship . . . were all considered . . . by the philosophers as equally false." Where the intelligentsia regards all religion as a spurious and irrelevant manifestation of the common people's superstition society is in trouble. The reason is that when thinkers formulate a culture's understanding of itself without regard for God you sever the roots of that culture and produce a "cut-flower" civilization which soon perishes. The record of man's attempts to build a lasting city for himself without reference to God has not been promising, from the Tower of Babel until now. Whenever we say that all religions are alike and that all are false we are no nearer the truth than when say that all are true.

But perhaps the most cynical view of all is that of Gibbon's magistrates who found "all modes of worship equally useful." Sometimes one fears that politicians, although they profess to abhor him, owe more to Karl Marx than they are willing to admit. He said that religion is the opium of the people. He saw it as the force that kept the masses deceived and therefore manageable by their masters. Whenever "magistrates," political figures, use the appeal of "God and country," one gets the uneasy feeling that they are perilously close to Gibbon's harsh judgment of Rome.

No, not all religions are the same, any more than all families are the same. Jesus said, "By their fruits you shall know them." Test the religion that knocks at your door in terms of what it has done to bring man to God and to unite him with his fellowman.

4

On Going and Getting There

Ask my children about good memories of growing up and both will describe two summer cross-country family vacations taken in an unairconditioned DeSoto. We had plenty of togetherness with six in the car and utensils for fixing most of our meals. Sometimes it was too much for irritated dispositions aggravated by the hot wind whistling through opened windows, or a child throwing up in the back seat. But we endured the discomfort in order to enjoy the objectives.

Immediate objective on a searing hot day would be an air-conditioned motel in the evening, with a swimming pool if we got lucky. More important objectives were sights and wonders all across this beautiful country. Marion is a trip-planner like you wouldn't believe, maximizing the miles. We saw more of America on those two trips

Life's Unexpected Dividends / 93

than I have seen the rest of my years combined. The memories still enrich us.

Both our then little girls fell in love with Yosemite National Park, resolving on the spot to return on their honeymoons, which neither got to do. But our living daughter and her husband have now taken their own two little girls to see Yosemite, and those little girls want to go back on their honeymoons.

Sometimes I think that my whole life has been a kind of extension of the vacation-trip motif. There have been immediate (or better, intermediate) objectives, a lot of them. Get an education, pastor a church, get the children safely grown and on their own, teach at the college level, write a book, meet a deadline, and so on.

Certain objectives had to be surrendered because they became unattainable. Some were abandoned because they became uninteresting or irrelevant before I ever got around to them. Early on we fantasized about running a motel when we retired. You know, "meet all those interesting people." It must have been about the time of those two cross-country trips. It would be called, "Sleepy Hollow Motel—A Family Place." Another time we were going to open a chili parlor.

The trips had an ultimate goal, to get home safely, which we did despite a couple of scares such as nearly getting wiped out one night in McCook, Nebraska. That applies to my life goal, too. I want to get safely home—tired, used up, full of rich memories.

The Bible uses the journey or pilgrimage metaphor a lot. "Abraham went out, not knowing whither he went." He didn't have Miriam to plan his itinerary. But he arrived safely in Canaan. "For you shall go out in joy,/and be led forth in peace" (Isa. 55:12), said God's prophet to the exiles traveling from Babylon's bondage to their Jerusalem home.

The same theme recurs in the New Testament. So Brother Paul wrote to some friends about some of his personal aspirations, adding: "The one thing I do, however, is to forget what is behind me and do my best to reach what is ahead. So I run straight toward the goal in order to win the prize, which is God's call through Christ Jesus to the life above" (Phil. 3:13-14, GNB).

In one of his letters, John expresses this life-process theme eloquently. "Beloved, we are God's children now; it does not yet appear what we shall be, but we know that when he appears we shall be like him, for we shall see him as he is" (1 John 3:2). In short, we already are somebody important—God's children—but we aren't fully grown children yet. We are working on it, or better, God is working on it in us.

Paul sees life the same way. We are "being changed into his likeness from one degree of glory to another; for this comes from the Lord who is the Spirit" (2 Cor. 3:18). But he can't get very far with us without our cooperation.

I really am committed to the concept of intermediate objectives combined with long-range goals. The intermediate objectives don't all have to be related, either to one another or to the ultimate goal. Some objectives are just for fun, like Robert Frost's, "The Road Not Taken." But they all have meaning to us, and they may bring us nearer the goal.

A student comes to see me because he suddenly wakes up to realize that he is a senior in college and still doesn't know what he wants to do with his life. He has just been enjoying getting to know himself and other people. Another student comes who is disturbed because he knows what he wants to do with his life, but he can see no way to get there from where he is.

The message to both is the same. Take hold where you are. Do something worthwhile this very day. Do another worthwhile thing tomorrow. The way will come clear. Don't miss today's sights because you are worrying about arriving at the ultimate destination. And don't be in such a hurry that you don't ever look into a child's eyes or touch somebody's hand.

IX
What Is the Bible to Us?

1

Once again the Bible is newsworthy and, on balance, I believe that it is a good thing. It sure beats the antics of Hollywood heroes and heroines as a topic for the evening news. I used to have an insurance salesman friend who liked to jest, "I don't care what you say about me as long as you mention my name." He figured that any news was better than no news at all.

People are taking the Bible very seriously, even choosing up sides. That isn't all bad. At least it shows that the Bible matters to them. What is destructive of Christian unity, what wounds the Body of Christ, is the tendency to absolutize one's own view of the Bible while condemning those who disagree with it. The line between faithfulness and fanaticism is thin. But on that theme you might write the entire history of Christendom.

In a recent sermon our pastor observed that many people seem to be worshiping the Bible, others appear to be ignoring it, while all of us ought to be listening to it. It was a good sermon (I haven't heard him preach a lackluster one) and I wouldn't alter a sentence except to wonder if those who make up the first two groups—the worshipers and the ignorers—aren't sometimes the same folks. Not all who do one are guilty of the other, to be sure, but neither honors the Scripture.

What shall we believe about the Bible? What we believe need not be limited to what we know, but it ought to bear some relationship to knowledge. For instance, we say: "The Bible is divinely inspired. God is its Author. He 'in-breathed' it." We may cite 2 Timothy 3:16 or perhaps 2 Peter 1:20-21 as our authority. For me that is authority enough. But then we begin to wonder just how God went about inspiring those who wrote the Bible.

Were they merely recorders, dictating machines, God giving them the very words in Hebrew for the Old Testament and Greek for the New? Many people seem to be saying that that is what they believe is meant by divine inspiration of Scripture. There is nothing in Scripture itself to suggest that God gave it word by word. People who hold the dictation theory of inspiration will likely respond: "I realize that the biblical documents we now have are not letter perfect, but I believe that the original manuscripts were dictated by God. I accept this on faith." Such a faith statement is unarguable, because it is not grounded in reason but is a faith commitment.

But not everyone who believes in the divine inspiration of Scripture believes the dictation theory of original manuscripts. That does not mean they love the Bible less, honor it less, or believe less in its divine origin and authority. Their faith commitment is that God spoke through the words of the writers of Scripture. The Bible is "the Word of God through the words of men," as someone has put it. We all believe that he has spoken fully and completely through his Son, Jesus Christ.

Such a view does not limit God's ability to speak his Word, but suggests that he used special gifts and traits of his chosen messengers to speak and write his divine message. Amos, though he lived and preached in the same time and place as Hosea, does not sound like Hosea but like himself. Matthew does not write like John and John does not use the thought forms of Paul. Is not the Word of God more miraculous because he did not turn the writers of the Bible into automatic typewriters, but used their individuality to express his infallible truth?

Furthermore, the Bible did not come together all at once, but through a long process of filtering. Other religions may claim that their sacred writings were miraculously delivered as finished products, but that may not be said of the Bible. It accumulated. By the end of the fifth century BC, the five books of Old Testament Law had been accepted as sacred. By 200 BC, the Old Testament books of prophecy had come to be regarded as Scripture. But not until the end of the first century AD was the Old Testament canon finalized.

The same process went on in the formation of the New Testament. In some early lists of New Testament books some of the present New Testament was omitted, such as James, Hebrews, and the Epistles of Peter. Other books, not now in the New Testament, were sometimes included. Only gradually, by general usage, by the self-authentication of the books that survived, did the New Testament become what it is to us today. The earliest official canon of the New Testament known to us today was issued in AD 387.

None of the above shadows the validity of the Bible as the divinely inspired record of God's revelation. What it does is to put the matter in an entirely different light than the one in which it is currently discussed in many places.

2

What We Owe to the Biblical Scholars

If you opened your Bible and read, "Nyl'yee deme, that yee be not demede, for in what dome yee demen, yee schulen be demede," you would probably suppose that the typesetter had fallen asleep over his keys. But in fact the words are John Wycliffe's 1382 English translation from Latin of Matthew 7:1-2: "Judge not, that you be not judged. For with the judgment you pronounce you will be judged."

Wycliffe's was the first English translation of the Bible. Both government and church sought to suppress it, certain that popularizing the Scripture would destroy its sacredness. Followers of Wycliffe, disparagingly called *Lollards,* a word that meant "mutterers," went about the country reading the Bible in Wycliffe's translation to common people who could not read it for themselves but were hungry for its words.

The irresistible force of God's Spirit spread the work of Bible translation into native languages like wildfire. On the Continent the brilliant Erasmus wrote on the eve of the Reformation, "I vehemently dissent from those who would not have private persons read the Holy Scriptures. . . . I wish they were translated into all languages of all peoples."

That wish is well on the way to being fulfilled, since there are now more than 1,500 such Bible translations. Thanks to the dedicated labors of hundreds and thousands of devout Bible scholars persons even in the remote areas of the globe can read the Scriptures in their native tongue. People who deride biblical scholarship only display their own ignorance, for it was the scholars who gave such persons the opportunity to read the Bible in the first place.

As the author of the Epistle to the Hebrews says about the roll of Old Testament heroes, "time would fail me" to call the complete roll of those who gave their labors, and sometimes their very lives, to the task of searching for the best text and then faithfully rendering it in language understandable to the common reader. If you know much of their story, you are not apt to be satisfied with doctrinaire pronouncements of suspicion of biblical scholarship.

Consider William Tyndale, trained at Oxford and Cambridge, who came to the conviction that it was "impossible to establish lay people in any truth except the scripture were plainly laid before their eyes in their mother tongue." Because of intense opposition, Tyndale fled to Germany where he produced the first English translation of the New Testament from its original language, Greek.

Copies of Tyndale's translation reached England in 1526 and were, as Edgar J. Goodspeed writes, "eagerly welcomed by people interested in the Reformation, but rigorously proscribed and sought out for destruction by the church authorities." So clear and powerful was Tyndale's translation that 92 per cent of the King James Version of the New Testament is still just as William Tyndale wrote it. He had said that he would make a version so plain a plowboy could read and understand, and he did. But it was not just simple; it reflected the scholar's fine touch and the marks of literary genius. For his labors Tyndale was hunted down, captured, and burned at the stake.

There were other martyrs to the cause of biblical scholarship, but suppression was impossible. By 1539 the so-called "Great Bible," a huge pulpit Bible in English, had appeared and soon was to be found in every parish church secured by a chain to the pulpit so that it could not be carried off by eager laypersons who were learning to read and wanted to read the Bible for themselves. And the work of translation goes on to this day.

Today's Bible scholar has more tools at his disposal than any of his predecessors. For one thing, he has available for his use manuscripts of the New Testament which date back to the fourth and fifth centuries AD. Other fragments of manuscripts which have come to light are even earlier and represent dramatic discoveries which add to the scholar's understanding and make his work of translation more exciting.

One of the most amazing discoveries was the Chester Beatty papyri found in Egypt in 1931 and containing, among other writings, the Gospels and Acts, the letters of Paul, and the Revelation. These texts date from the second, third, and fourth centuries AD. The work of searching, analyzing, evaluating, and translating goes on and on. There are now some 6,000 manuscripts and fragments of the New Testament at the scholars' disposal.

Through all of this labor God is using the intelligent skill of devoted men and women to give us his Word in words that are plain to us.

3

The Biblical Writers as Real People

Emerson once went to hear a preacher and reported later that the man's sermon was so impersonal you couldn't tell if the preacher had ever been tempted, had ever sinned, had ever loved, laughed or wept, or looked into an open grave. His preaching may have been theologically sound but it was personally lifeless.

Such could never be said about the writers of the Bible. They were not automatic typewriters impersonally clacking into print the words of a programmed message. They were people fired by a divine vision filtered through their individualities and expressed in the contexts of their personal experience. You can tell by the way they wrote where they were coming from.

For example, the Gospel of Mark reads like an eyewitness account. An ancient tradition held that the Book of Mark consists of the recollections of Simon Peter told to Mark during the closing years of Peter's life in Rome. Nobody can prove that, but the style of Mark is visual. He paints pictures. He describes Jesus as having the people sit down on "the green grass" in groups of hundreds and fifties to be fed. "Immediately" is one of his favorite words. His writing gives the feeling of action and movement.

While much of Mark's Gospel is incorporated in Matthew, they are quite different in many respects. Matthew was certain that the Hebrew Scriptures (our Old Testament) clearly indicated that Jesus of Nazareth is the promised Messiah. From start to finish he cited the Scripture to validate the claim that Jesus is the Christ. This was a characteristic of Matthew's style.

Other indications that Matthew had a scholar's mind are the arrangements of teaching materials in his Gospel. Five "mini-books" of teaching may be found in Matthew—chapters 5—7; 10; 13; 18; 24—25. Each of these five discourses of Jesus is concluded with the same saying: "And when Jesus finished. . . ." In his systematic arrangement, Matthew inserts the teaching materials between narratives of Jesus' ministry.

Luke explains in the introduction to his Gospel that he is a second generation Christian. He acknowledges that "many have undertaken to compile a narrative" of the events of Jesus Christ. His reason for writing another narrative is to set down "an orderly account" of what happened just as it was reported by those who were "eyewitnesses and ministers of the word."

A Gentile, Luke seems unfamiliar with Palestinian geography. He writes in good Greek style with a minimum of Hebrew words and expressions, and emphasizes the wider, more universal aspects of the Gospel. Luke stresses Jesus' concern for the poor, the outcast, the

What Is the Bible to Us? / 101

Samaritan, and for women and children. His is a Gospel to encourage the dispossessed.

John, the fourth Gospel, stands apart from the others. While they are so similar that they have been called "The Synoptic Gospels," meaning that they "see" alike, John is distinct. He begins with a theological declaration about the eternal existence of Christ, the Word. He reports an early ministry of Jesus in Judea, whereas the Synoptics report that Jesus began in Galilee. John reports three visits of Jesus to Jerusalem to attend the Passover whereas the others mention only one. John places the driving of the money changers from the Temple at the beginning of Jesus' ministry, whereas the others have it at the end.

But the most distinctive difference in John is his use of Jesus' miraculous works as "signs" or evidences of his divine nature. John sees a spiritual and symbolic meaning to what happened. For this reason, since the third century, John's has been called "the spiritual Gospel."

If we turn from the Gospel writers to Paul, who wrote more of the New Testament than any other man, we see the same personal distinctives that have been observed in the Gospels. Paul writes with his own distinctive style as an educated Jew who is proud of his Jewish heritage and who also regards his Roman citizenship as a prized possession. He is a man totally caught up in his personal experience with Christ and wholly committed to share what he understands to be the nature of salvation with all who will hear him.

Read Paul and you will encounter some central themes reiterated throughout his letters. One of these is the universal sway of sin and its consequences, spiritual death. Another is the ineffectual nature of good works as a means of redemption. A companion thought is the justification of all persons who will commit themselves in faith to Christ as Lord.

The point of this cursory look at some of the writers in the New Testament is that each is a distinctive individual whose individuality comes through the writing which he has left us under the inspiration of God's Holy Spirit. For their individual contribution to the one and only gospel of God's redemptive love we are indebted.

4

God Finishes What He Starts

"Don't start what you can't finish," a little boy warns his opponent as they square off on the school grounds at recess. Unless taunted into swinging at one another by the ever-present circle of wiseacres eager to see somebody else fight, both boys may manage to save face and bloody noses by neither striking the first blow before the bell rings. Pray God that will happen between us and the Russians.

Of course, finishing what you start is a mark of good character. Many a person's life is a trail of half-done jobs. He never sees anything through to completion—not his marriage or job or friendships or personal growth or his relationship with the Lord. Life becomes a succession of starts and fizzles.

I do not want to write today about our inconstancy, but about God's constancy. Basic to my faith and to my ability to cope with everything happening to me and around me is assurance that God always, one way or another, finishes what he begins. I am counting on that, and with what I submit is good reason.

This is not to suggest that God is an irresistible Cosmic Necessity, making whatever happens simply another case of God getting his way. We can't equate the morning paper's headlines with God's will without making him responsible for unspeakable enormities. Nor does this mean that God never loses anything he made. Dinosaurs are no longer with us, not as dinosaurs, anyway. What this claim—that God finishes what he starts—does mean is that he is going to bring the creation to the conclusion to which he intended it from the beginning. He didn't set out to build a Temple and wind up building a slaughterhouse and a brothel. He isn't finished yet.

If I understand the Bible, this is what it is saying. A theme runs through the music of its various parts of time, place, and perspective. God's purpose to redeem what he created is this theme. God is in the reclamation business. He is in the process of claiming and shaping all

What Is the Bible to Us? / 103

reality—that which is in us, around us, and beyond us to the farthest reaches of being. It is an ongoing project whose end we do not yet see.

There is no question that Scripture witnesses to this cosmic intention of the Creator-Redeemer. Such thoughts occupy Paul's mind as he writes to the Christians at Rome about God's long-range program: "All of creation waits with eager longing for God to reveal his sons. . . . Yet there was the hope that creation itself would one day be set free from its slavery to decay and would share the glorious freedom of the children of God. For we know that up to the present time all of creation groans with pain, like the pain of childbirth" (Rom. 8:19-22, GNB).

Something like childbirth is happening to the creation! This vivid metaphor captures the imagination of the apostle as he searches his mind to express what he thinks is going on. There is pain in childbirth —and struggle, too, and uncertainty, and risk. We know of the mother's pain. She can tell us about it. But we now are beginning to appreciate the trauma experienced by the baby being born. We cannot assume that there is no self-consciousness in the baby, that because he is unable to tell us of his pain there is none.

But the other side of the pain of birth is far more important. That is the expectancy and the joy of new life. God is birthing a new world, Paul is bold enough to imply. It is a hazardous, painful, and terribly long process, but he knows what he is doing and he plans to see it through.

Over in 2 Peter, which may have been the last of the New Testament writings, there is consolation for people who love God but wonder what he is up to. Second Peter was written to such folks. "The Lord is not slow to do what he has promised" (3:9, GNB), the writer reassures. The problem is that we want him to do it on our schedule, and he doesn't operate that way. "There is no difference in the Lord's sight between one day and a thousand years; to him the two are the same" (v. 9, GNB). God has his own timetable, and he won't be hurried by our impatience.

I see considerable evidence that God hasn't ditched us and gone off to do something else. He hasn't given up on us. Let us not give up on ourselves. Some years ago a student friend of mine who had spent a lot of hours in my office talking about some problems, left me a plaque I prize. On it are these words: "Please be patient—God hasn't finished with me yet." Not yet—nor tomorrow—nor next year will he be finished with us. Keep on working at letting him bring you to fullness of life.

5

In Praise of Reading and Writing

Four thousand years ago an Egyptian father, sailing south on the Nile to enroll his son in a school for scribes, told the boy: "It is to writings that you must set your mind. I do not see an office to be compared with that of scribe. I shall make you love books more than your mother, and I shall place their excellence before you."

Writing already had a long tradition in Egypt when that father praised it to his son. Between five and six thousand years ago the Egyptians were using writing for communication and preservation of records. While our Hebrew ancestors were still chasing goats over desert sand dunes, the Egyptians had accumulated a long cultural history.

Today's popular wisdom is contemptuous of learning. What do you need writing for, other than to cash your paycheck? As for reading books, that is a last resort. Television has made reading obsolete in many American homes. If you don't believe it, ask your schoolteachers. They will tell you that the number of young people who can neither write a complete sentence nor read one longer than ten monosyllabic words is appalling.

A few years back I was catching a morning flight and discovered that a well-known college basketball team was on the plane. They had played our college team the night before and I had seen the game and been impressed by the basketball talents of two of the opposing players who are now in big bucks in the NBA. Getting aboard, I sat down beside a fine-looking young man who immediately got out his chemistry book. Across the aisle from us sat these two superstars who, as soon as we took off, broke out their comic books. My chemistry-studying seatmate was a sub who didn't get to play the night before. According to the popular wisdom he had better study his chemistry if he wants to make a living, but they could sit back and enjoy their comic books. Somebody would take care of their academic eligibility until they used up their four years of college basketball, they then would become instant millionaires, thereafter riding around in their Rolls Royces and answering TV interviewers with that profound all-American declaration, "You know."

To be sure, there are exceptions. Bill Bradley, All-American at Princeton, was also a Rhodes Scholar, a subsequent NBA millionaire, and now a United States senator. This column is not a peevish put-down of college athletics. I am an avid fan. It is one person's dismay over the decline in appreciation of reading and writing, the low regard we have for learning. Even bright youth are brainwashed by this society to demand that their education "prepare them for a profession," which means "guarantee to help you make a lot of money."

Maybe that Egyptian father was a bit extreme when he told his boy he was going to make him "love books more than your mother," but not many among us are likely to become book freaks. Our tastes in language, music, and the visual arts point instead to a return to primitivism. Do you ever pay attention to the songs your children hear twenty times a day by car radio and evening television? "She was easy as pie," is a current ennobling example.

Does it seem significant to you that the average American high school graduate has spent 15,000 hours of his life watching TV, while only 11,000 hours in formal schooling? Does it seem important that by the time of his high school graduation he will have been subjected to 640,000 TV commercials? Then you will send him off to college and demand that somebody educate him.

Let's hear it for learning to read and write—and spell. A student complains about a professor's grade. "He took off points for a few little mistakes like misspelled words!" Good for him. It is not "picky" to demand that a college student be reasonably literate. Occasionally it may appear to be hopeless.

How turn this around? I'm not much for censorship. Censors have a way of wanting you to read or hear only what they decide is good for you. As soon as newspapers and magazines all stop publishing due to the lamentable fact that there are no more Americans who can read anything more complex than a comic book we shall be altogether dependent upon the marvelous gift of TV to show and tell us all we know. Maybe they can hire gifted readers to read the great books of our past to us on TV. Then perhaps some bright child will say to its mother, "Mama, I want to learn to do that for myself."

God has given us the most valuable Book, in my view. I owe it much. It comforts, chastises, humbles, and enheartens me. It gives me hope. I do not know it well, but I know it better than any other book. It speaks a relevant word to me about everything I experience, for it has an inspired timelessness which makes it the Book for all seasons. I can't imagine how impoverished life would be for me without the Bible.

X
Coping with the Shadow

1

Between auspicious beginnings and ordinary endings a lot of things happen. T. S. Eliot wrote about the slippage between departure and arrival, referring to the world ending "not with a bang but a whimper." In the same poem he repeated the words, "Falls the Shadow!"

I have strong aversion to the "whimper syndrome." Please kick me if you catch me at it. While I am not so naive as to believe in the "ever onward and upward" nonsense of many contemporary self-help schemes, neither am I so cynical and despairing as to suppose that all idealism, vitality, and aspiration turn out to be impossible dreams and wind up in a sigh, or worse, a whine.

But the Shadow—ah, that is something else again. Whoever supposes that he will make it through life in the sunshine and never encounter the darkness of the Shadow is kidding himself. The Shadow is real. Perhaps the best known and loved of all the Psalms talks about that reality: "Yea, though I walk through the valley of the shadow of death, I will fear no evil, for thou art with me. Thy rod and thy staff, they comfort me" (23:4, KJV). Are you acquainted with the Shadow?

It takes many forms—death of a loved person; bitter disappointment in a relationship; failure in business; emotional and spiritual depression; threat to one's own health and survival. The one thing you can count on is that somewhere, sometime, you will meet up with the Shadow. What do you do then? The answer you give may well determine when or if you come out of the experience a whole person.

Probably the first thing to do is to resist the temptation to believe that you have been singled out for special persecution and suffering. We are prone to believe when we are in the Shadow that we are victims of a cosmic plot hatched by Whoever or Whatever determines human fate. Don't give in to that. Even in the Bible examples of this sort of paranoid response to trouble exist. That is what happened to Job when he was at his most despairing time. He concluded that God really had it in for him and had organized some kind of scheme to destroy him. One of the lessons he had to learn was that he was taking himself much too seriously when he supposed that God had picked on him.

When you are engulfed in the Shadow, you need to do a second thing. Keep moving. If you sit down and wait for the Shadow to go away, for the fog to lift, you may be sitting there a long time, perhaps even for the rest of your life. The idea will never turn into the reality, the motion will never become the act, the conception will never become a creation, and the emotion will never elicit the needed response—not if you just sit there. As they say, "Do something, even if it's wrong." Or as that great black baseball pitcher and philosopher, Satchel Paige, was fond of saying, "Don't look back—something may be gaining on you."

Keep moving, but don't just engage in random activity. Movement for the sake of movement, to give the appearance that you are going somewhere when actually all you are doing is running in place—or in circles—is self-defeating and self-deceiving.

Ask for help. Somebody can help you push the spider web of Shadow far enough away from your face to be able to take the first step, then the second, and another and another, until you get through the Shadow to the light. A saying I like goes, "Faith is walking to the edge of all the light you can see and then taking one more step." I sometimes paraphrase that to read, "Faith is walking carefully but purposefully to the edge of all the Shadow that engulfs you, until you begin to see and recognize the light."

If you do take that first step, then the second, and so on, you are going to be in for some great surprises, most of them pleasant. I understand the feeling of being in the Shadow. It is scary. Shadow creeps inside your clothes, penetrates your pores, burns your nostrils when you try to breathe. Claustrophobia closes in. I know about that.

But if you keep walking, you are going to encounter some wonderful people and places. And, what is more, eventually you will emerge from the Shadow with the idea become a reality you never dreamed of, the motion changed into an act you never anticipated, the conception into a wholly unexpected creation.

God is always leading us into good surprises. He led Abraham to a homeland, Joseph to the prime ministership of Egypt through the Shadow of slavery and imprisonment, Moses to be deliverer of his people through being raised in Pharaoh's house, and David from being a shepherd to the throne of Judah and Israel. Maybe God has a sense of humor. Who knows what lies on the other side of the Shadow for you?

Remember: "Yea, though I walk through the valley of the shadow, . . . Thou art with me."

2

Dying Before You Live

Dying is not the worst thing that can happen. The worst is to go out of the world without ever having learned any reason to be in it. Solzhenitsyn said in his poem, "The First Circle," that people "waste themselves in senseless thrashing around for the sake of a handful of goods and die without realizing their spiritual wealth." Instead of "goods," he could have said "power," "prestige," or "pleasure," and it would have been as true. How sad to die without ever a clue about why you were alive.

Do you ever think about what makes life good? One thing for me is an increasing sense of wonder and joy in the commonplace. Children know this, but growing up scales the eyes and hardens the arteries of the spirit so that we no longer see and sense the wonder of life in the ordinary. Maybe we have to be battered a bit and aged a lot before we reawaken the wonder within us.

Shall I confide in you some of the extraordinary commonplaces of my present life? The friendship of students, the satisfaction of writing this piece week in and week out, the voice of one of my grandchildren over long distance saying, "I love you, Pop," the discovery of new meaning in an old text. Those are some of the things that make life good for me.

Another part of learning to live is encouraging the art of saying hello and goodbye. There is an art to saying both. Purposeful living includes being open enough to accept the gifts of human relationship and mature enough to relinquish them when the time comes to do so.

This is not to say that one should not expect to have any long-term relationships. It is to observe that life is by nature a pilgrimage, and that there is a time to make camp and a time to break camp. There are those who go through life afraid to give themselves to any genuine relationship for fear of getting hurt when the time comes to move on. So they travel alone, preferring loneliness to the risk of the pain of a lost relationship.

People who have learned how to live work to make the most of every occasion and every relationship, knowing that the good stuff is held by a tenuous thread. One savors what life gives, surrendering it sadly but not resentfully when it is time, knowing that no experience is ever really lost but that it abides as a part of oneself.

Further, one experiences through faith the reality of other life-satisfying moments—moments which do not take the place of what is lost, but bring their own unique gift. So, like children moving from hand to hand through a line of dancers in an old-fashioned Virginia reel, we surrender one safety island of life at the moment of reaching out to another.

People suffering the acute grief of a permanent loss often feel that the pain is both unbearable and unending. But it is neither. Eventually the pain is absorbed into every nook and cranny of one's being, becoming an intrinsic part of one's personhood and perspective. To let that happen and not to become bitter in the process, is surely one of life's greatest achievements.

An important ingredient in the satisfying life is realizing that I only need to be who I am, and that I am not responsible to be anybody else. I have an awful time with that one. This is not to say that I need to make no changes in my life. What it does mean is that I don't have to depend upon excelling according to other people's standards in order to be somebody. I am somebody. You may wish I were different from the way I am. In some ways, I do, too, but this is who I am.

In his book, *To Kiss the Joy,* Robert Raines tells of visiting a pastor and his family where there were three sons, two extremely bright and the third terribly retarded. Upon leaving, Raines asked if he might take a family picture, assuming that it would include the parents and two boys. But the father said, "Just a moment. I'll have to get him ready," pointing to the twenty-year-old man with a child's mind. And when the picture was taken there he was, sitting right in front between his brothers.

God does not ask if you are bright or witty or rich or famous or powerful or good looking. He only wants you to be in the family picture because you are his and you belong with your brothers.

One thing I have noticed about living a satisfying life is that those whose lives seem fullest do not seem preoccupied with the need to make their lives full. They are so busy living and being concerned about how other people are making it that they do not appear to have time to count their own happiness pulse. Happiness almost appears to be a happening.

William Blake put it succinctly: "He who binds to himself a joy Does the winged life destroy." To this Robert adds: "If we hug our happiness to ourselves, . . . one day we wake up to discover we're hugging a corpse."

3

The Two Wash Basins

A folk song about war says that if you make up your mind to fight and kill other people, don't blame it on God. That makes me want to re-examine not only our sanction of war, but also of just about anything we decide to do.

Recently I heard a sermon that raised the same issue. The preacher contrasted the use of two basins of water referred to in the Gospels. With one Jesus had washed his disciples' feet as an act of service and love. With the other Pontius Pilate had washed his hands of responsibility for Jesus' death.

The preacher made the point that everybody has the option to use the basin in one way or the other. Some take it to love and serve, while others habitually employ it as a means of excusing themselves from personal responsibility.

Sad to say, most of us are more kin to Pilate than to Jesus, although we call him Lord. If Pilate were the guest columnist today, he would probably represent himself as one of history's most misjudged characters.

Think what his defense might be: "I didn't have anything against that Galilean preacher. He seemed like a decent sort, a bit weird, with notions about forgiving one's enemies, love and brotherhood, and something he called the kingdom of God, but plainly no threat to Rome.

"Further," Pilate would write, "I didn't want to come to Palestine in the first place. Everybody in the Roman civil service knew that it was no man's land for the aspiring public servant. I can't tell you how many good men were ruined politically by that job.

"The people were not easy subjects to rule. From the first they were after me, always reporting to my superiors some insult or slight to their religion.

"That day they demanded the crucifixion of the Galilean preacher I tried everything I could think of to avoid bloodshed. I could have called out the riot squad and broken a few heads, but it wouldn't have settled anything. It seemed better to give them what they demanded.

"Maybe I was wrong, but how can you judge me? You were not there. So I washed my hands of the matter. It wasn't my fault. I was only a civil servant doing my duty, trying to keep the peace with as little violence as possible. Would you have done differently? I doubt it."

Well, that is Pilate's defense. Do you buy it? But come closer home, for the same kind of moral issues confront us. No event in this century evoked greater moral indignation than the Nazi systematic extermination of European Jews. But multitudes of good, God-fearing people sat by and let it happen. I recoil in horror at the pictures of the gas chambers, but if I had been living in the area where one of these was operating, I wonder if I would have risked my life to protest. I suspect that I would have used Pilate's basin instead of Christ's. After all, I have managed to be fairly comfortable with a good deal of social injustice in my own country.

I wonder what those of you who will be alive a quarter of a century from now will say when your children or grandchildren ask you, "What did you do when your government was pulverizing Vietnam into one huge trash heap?" I predict that you will answer: "Well, you see, I was in college then and didn't have anything to do with it," or "I was just an ordinary citizen with no voice in the government." Or maybe you will say, "Our nation got drawn into that disaster and just couldn't find any way out. It wasn't our fault." Let me hand you Pilate's basin. Jesus' would get you hurt.

It is so very easy to talk about morality from a safe distance. History has judged Pilate. It doesn't require a lot of courage to say that he should have acted like a statesman instead of a politician. But it is quite another thing to talk about making courageous moral decisions which involve your courage and morality.

A for instance comes to mind. Some years ago a student was lamenting what he considered to be the lack of moral indignation in the country over the Watergate scandal. I asked if it would be appropriate to bring the problem closer home. Were students outraged when professors' offices were rifled at exam times and copies of exams stolen? Was that a parallel moral issue?

No wave of moral revulsion swept over the group of students present. In fact, nobody said a word. After a moment, one student said, "Well, let's get back to the subject. Now, about Watergate. . . ."

This is not to excuse Pilate's callousness, Hitler's cruelty, or the conspiracy of Watergate. It is to make a plea for personal responsibility in matters over which we have some control. I may not forestall international thievery and mass murder, but I sure can do something about my larcenous and hate-filled heart.

Of all the Pilate performances that go on none is more deplorable to me than the pious attribution to God's will of everything that happens. As the song says, "Don't blame it on God." Stand up, be a person charged with the dignifying task of taking responsibility for the kind of person you intend to be.

4

A Time to Mourn—A Time to Dance

The mother of an eighteen-year-old girl killed in a car wreck on Christmas Eve read my book, *The Morning After Death,* and wrote to me about her grief. She sent me Sherri's picture "so you will understand how beautiful she was." Could I help her with "Why"? Could I tell her when the hurt would stop being so deep? Could I tell her how to manage?

I answered, and she wrote back: "We had some classes at our church on grief after this happened to us and it is surprising how little people know. One lady said to me if I would put it all in the Lord's hands I would not have to suffer this way. She said some people cry at the least little thing. . . . She has never lost a child."

How can someone who has never lost a child have the effrontery to tell someone who has how to handle losing a child? Better and more honest would have been an embrace that said, "Please know I love you. I have no word except that I believe God loves you, too. I have not walked where you walk, but I can understand that you are crushed. I bear you up on my prayers to God, and I am sure that he is with you in your grief."

Sometimes grieving is about all you can manage. Qoheleth in Ecclesiastes says that "there is a time to mourn, and a time to dance."

Both are appropriate at the appropriate moment. The death of your child, especially on Christmas Eve, is a time to mourn. Call off the dance. Hopefully, there will again be a time when you will feel like dancing, but not now.

"We grieve," wrote Paul, "but not as those who have no hope" (1 Thess. 4:13, author's translation). It is not grief that is unbecoming to a Christian, but hopeless grief. Grief can be destructive if it is denied. Whoever, to show that he or she is a Christian or a mature person, refuses to allow himself to mourn is apt later to find himself loaded with an unbearable weight of unresolved grief.

Show me a brittle, hard person, or one constantly berating himself, or chronically depressed, and I will show you someone who likely has not dealt with a grief situation. Jesus' words in the Sermon on the Mount have new meaning for me in the light of my own griefs: "Blessed are those who mourn, for they shall be comforted" (Matt. 5:4). The ones not too proud to mourn get the comfort; those who refuse to mourn remain uncomforted. If you refuse to mourn, you may never feel like dancing again.

Psalm 30 addresses this need in the rich imagery of Hebrew poetry. The poet has been in the pit of despair, but God has drawn him out. Like all the rest of us, he had gone along blithely assuming that life would always be good: "I said in my prosperity, 'I shall never be moved'" (v. 6). Suddenly life collapsed about him; he was overcome. "O Lord my God, I cried to thee for help, and thou hast healed me. Thou hast turned my mourning into dancing" (v. 11, author's translation).

If we let God help us, he will turn our mourning into dancing, too. But we have to get to the place of being willing for him to do that for us. In your mourning you may not be ready yet. If not, that is all right provided you do not settle permanently in the state of grief. "Weeping may tarry for the night," sang the psalmist, "but joy comes with the morning" (30:5). Maybe it is still night in your heart. But don't try to hold back the morning, anymore than you refused to entertain the night of weeping.

God will help us through the night and into the morning by empowering us through grief to surrender those from whom we are separated. We have to give them up. Having fully expressed our sorrow, anger, despair, loneliness, and all the other honest emotions connected with such a loss, we say, "Now that is done. Now I must begin again. Now I resume my life, a scarred veteran with an added dimension to my capacity to care for other people."

God will help us to turn mourning into dancing by using grief as a teacher. Most of what we know is learned the hard way. Through grief we learn about the fragility of life, the vulnerability of our loved ones and of ourselves. What we love most dearly we hold by a slender thread.

But we also learn that God's grace is sufficient. Day by day in unpredictable ways he provides what we have to have in order to survive. Imperceptibly but certainly, the grief is absorbed, becoming a part of one's entire being, affecting all one thinks and does, hopefully mellowing and enriching all one is.

In 1829 the German theologian-pastor Friedrich Schleiermacher stood at the grave of his nine-year-old son, Nathanael, and prayed: "Now, thou God who art love, . . . make even this grievous trial a new blessing for me in my vocation! For me and all of mine let this communal pain become wherever possible a new bond of still more intimate love, and let it issue in a new apprehension of thy Spirit in all my household!"

Let us not refuse to weep in the night, nor reject joy in the morning.

XI
Time to Spare for God

1

"Blessed are those who are glad to have time to spare for God," wrote Thomas a' Kempis in the fifteenth-century classic, *The Imitation of Christ*. If true then, how much more so now. Happy are those who, in the whirlwind of activity of contemporary life, find time for God. But more, blessed are those who are glad to have time to spare for God. So often, time for God is a grudging, graceless gift. "You mean I've got to go to church again? Oh, no!"

One of the worst admissions we can make in our crazy world is that we have nothing to do. It's a worse affliction than athlete's foot or acne. Nothing to do? That is a dreaded specter. So we program our lives to be sure the time will never come when we have nothing to do.

The freshman girl or boy in the dormitory can imagine no condemnation worse than to find themselves facing a weekend with nothing to do. The busy executive feels guilty if he suddenly catches himself sitting reflectively without a telephone or dictaphone in his hand. The worker facing retirement worries about whether his collection of hobbies will take up all his time. We are terrified by unprogrammed time.

One of the impressive facts about Jesus is the balance in his life between programmed and unprogrammed time. Follow his schedule through the gospel stories and you will be impressed that he led an active, vigorous life. Yet you have the sense that he is in command of himself and of his situation. He "runs his job rather than allowing his job to run him."

Think of the occasions when the Gospels report that he turned aside for rest and prayer. On one such occasion he welcomed his disciples back after having sent them out on a mission. Upon returning, they reported to him all that they had done and taught. His response at the close of that report was to take them out of service for a period of rest and relaxation. "Come away by yourselves to a lonely place," he said, "and rest a while." Mark's Gospel, where this incident is reported, adds an interesting observation: "For many were coming and going, and they had no leisure even to eat" (Mark 6:31).

Think about how Jesus perceived the disciples' needs after their period of activity. Perhaps there are clues here for us. Notice that his was a prescription for their bodies—they needed time to rest. If you are dragging around physically exhausted, the chances of clear thinking and good decision making are severely diminished. Jesus knew that about the disciples. They needed time out from doing even God's work. Jesus was implying that rest, as well as service, is a holy order.

They needed not only time for rest but for reflection. There was not leisure in which to eat. If you watched the Pope moving through the swarms of admirers eager to touch him or be touched by him, to catch his eye, or to receive some indication of being acknowledged, you must have sensed not only the enormous energy such a dynamic spiritual figure generates in a crowd, but also the draining, consuming strain it puts upon his physical and spiritual strength.

Jesus must have experienced that again and again. Once a woman with a disease touched him as he was passing. The Gospels tell us that she was healed, but Jesus stopped, aware that her healing had cost him something. Thus it is that he takes his disciples away for a time of reflection. They needed to get their minds and bodies back together.

This time away was a period of reassessment, a reordering of their life and work. I know people who appear to be wandering aimlessly through life like some poor amnesia victim, pushed from day to day, place to place, crisis to crisis, never quite catching on to their identity and place. "Time to spare for God" is a fitting prescription for many a harassed victim of our rootless and displaced society. You could not successfully operate your business without a plan and without an audit or inventory. Why should we suppose that we can successfully live our lives without time for reflection?

But the time away was also a time for reassurance. Although they had achieved good results on their mission, opposition to Jesus' kingdom was growing steadily. Daily it was becoming more hazardous to be identified with him. John the Baptist had already lost his head. What was to happen to these followers of the One who shortly would tell them that he was going to Jerusalem to be crucified? They needed to be reassured.

Time for God can provide us the opportunity for rest, reflection, and reassurance. It can help us get our lives in focus. Are you glad to give God some of your time?

2

The Levels of Caring

"In the sense in which a man can ever be said to be at home in the world, he is at home not through dominating, or explaining, or appreciating, but through caring and being cared for," writes Milton Mayeroff. Not only is caring and being cared for the clue to being at home in the world, it is also the clue to being at home with God.

In one of his most endearing metaphors, Jesus called himself "the good shepherd (who) lays down his life for the sheep" (John 10:11). Caring distinguishes the behavior of the shepherd from that of the hired man. When the wolf attacks the flock the hired man does not place his body between the wolf and the sheep. Instead, he runs away. He runs, Jesus said, because he is a hired man and "cares nothing for the sheep."

To whatever degree we really care, not simply using concern for others as a veiled way of controlling them, we are like God who so loved the world that he gave his only begotten Son for it. But, of course, we are not God. We aren't even very much like God. Our caring, as our knowledge, is in part. We care selectively and fragmentally.

I believe that there are at least three discernible levels of caring. The first is the willingness to be inconvenienced. That is a test many of us fail. We will not put ourselves out for others, even to suffer minor inconvenience.

One reads the Gospels with astonishment at Jesus' inexhaustible patience with being imposed upon. He looked upon the crowds and saw them harrassed and helpless, "like sheep without a shepherd." No doubt many came to see him only out of curiosity. Some came perhaps because they had nothing better to do. Some came in the hope of free lunch.

"Send them away," his disciples advised him one day when he found himself surrounded by a crowd of 5,000 hungry people. I know the disciples' feeling. Don't you? "Tell those people to let us alone. They're bothering us."

One of Jesus' most devastating parables features a rich man who ignored a beggar named Lazarus lying at his gate. There is no hint that the rich man abused the beggar, set the dogs on him, or had him arrested and dragged off to jail for loitering. He just let the beggar be. Indeed, the beggar subsisted on crumbs which fell from the rich man's table. But the crumbs cost the rich man nothing. They were thrown out anyway. The rich man suffered no inconvenience.

The second level of caring is willingness to become involved. That is a step beyond being inconvenienced. I may tolerate inconvenience as long as I am not asked to get involved. That is the reason, Jesus said, why the hired man runs when the wolf attacks. The sheep are not his; he has no investment in their welfare. Why should he care? It's not his problem.

The widow of Samuel Barnett, a man who spent his life improving conditions in the slums of London's East End, wrote after her husband's death that those who came down from the fashionable West End with large plans for the redemption of the dreary slums did little good. Only those "who were willing to take time and trouble with individuals" did any permanent good. To be sure.

There is a marvelous verse in Exodus about this. "One day when Moses had grown up," the Scripture reads, "he went out to his people and looked on their burdens" (2:11). It was then that he realized he could no longer accept the protection of living as the Egyptian king's son. He was an Israelite, and he had to get involved in their plight.

The highest level of caring is identification. At this level the other's plight has become our own. We are not only willing to be inconvenienced, and we are not only involved, but his cause has become our cause, his need our need.

A poet expressed this level of caring when he wrote:

> A man was starving in Capri.
> He moved his eyes and looked at me.
> I felt his gaze, I heard his moan,
> And I knew his hunger as my own.
> I saw at sea a great fog bank,
> Between two ships that struck and sank.
> A thousand screams the heavens smote,
> And every scream tore through my throat.
>
> AUTHOR UNKNOWN

To identify fully with others belongs only to God. That is what we Christians mean by Incarnation. God did not love us by remote control. He did not see us drowning and stand on the bank cupping his hands and calling out instructions on how to swim. He came to our side to rescue us. He joined us in our plight in this world, becoming one with us.

We cannot do that fully, perhaps not even for those whom we love most, not even our own flesh and blood. But we are called to care, and we can care if we will allow ourselves to be inconvenienced, to become involved, and to identify with others' condition.

3

The Priority of Persons

One night, many years ago, two of the foremost philosophers of the English-speaking world spent an evening together. One was Professor John Fiske of Harvard. The other was the celebrated English thinker and writer, Herbert Spencer, whose claims for the automatic progress

122 / Images of Eternity

of mankind through an evolutionary process profoundly influenced nineteenth-century Western thought.

The two had passed the hours in Spencer's home enjoying a discussion of their common interest, philosophy. As the evening drew to a close, Spencer asked Fiske about his family and Fiske did what any proud parent is apt to do—got out his wallet and showed his host a picture.

That night Fiske wrote his wife as follows: "I showed Spencer the little picture of our picnic-wagon with the children inside. When I realized how lonely he must be without any wife and babies of his own, and how solitary he is in all his greatness, I had to pity him. Then as I watched him studying that picture and gazing at our children's faces I said to myself, *That wagon-load of youngsters is worth more than all the philosophy ever concocted, from Aristotle to Spencer inclusive.*"

How do you react to that? Maybe you question whether a wagon load of children is worth that much, but if it were a wagon load of your children or grandchildren I doubt that you would have any problem about the question. Unless you are a most unusual person, that vignette reaches you deep in the heart and reflects an instinctive feeling—persons are all-important.

But there is more than instinct—"the mother fights to the death to defend her young"—here. The higher one gets in the scale of being the more sensitive one is to the worth and rights of persons. Thus the instinctive urge to protect one's own young is cultivated to include the young and defenseless of others in our tribe. Then this concern for others matures further until it includes the defenseless among our enemies. Ultimately, according to Jesus, the process of becoming God-like would cause us to embrace the whole human race as our family, making us put the welfare of any person above abstract ideas or material things.

Think how much Jesus made of this principle. He never spoke of issues as if they were somehow separate from the well-being of persons. He did not engage in philosophical games. He wasn't much for theological argumentation. He never alluded to God as if he were an object or principle to be defined, or an idea to be comprehended.

Does one want to know about God? Well, said Jesus, a certain man had two sons. One of them ran off to a far country and squandered his life in riotousness. The other stayed home and pouted and sulked. But the father loved them both with an undiminished and impartial concern, whether they were prodigals afar or at home. That is the way God loves.

Does one want to know how to be a neighbor? Well, said Jesus, a man was going from Jerusalem to Jericho when he fell among robbers who beat him and left him half dead. Two religious persons came along that road but, upon seeing the victim, passed on by without helping. Then came a Samaritan, member of a despised race thought incapable of sensitivity, and he stopped beside the victim and attended his wounds. Not satisfied with having given first-aid, the Samaritan further involved himself by getting the wounded Jew to a hostel, obligating himself for the stranger's bed and board. You can talk until you are blue in the face about neighborliness. You can have committee meetings and organize friendly get-togethers around the barbecue grill. But real neighborliness is expressed in person-to-person acts.

I am haunted when I allow myself to take the words of Jesus seriously. He tells me that my eternal life hangs upon whether I acknowledged and served "one of the least of these my brothers." The words astonish me. It is not whether I made the correct propositional confession of faith, or whether I was baptized with the right amount of water in the prescribed manner by the proper authority, or whether I belonged to the true church, or whether I even went to church. Did I love and serve Christ? Only if I saw him in the eyes of the least of his brothers and sisters. I stand under conviction.

If persons are so important, I must examine my priorities. I must forego the temptation to categorize people. I must revise my easy-going way of dealing with issues, hiding behind "the principle of the thing" when I want to run roughshod over another's rights or feelings. I must be more careful about using people while sanctimoniously intoning the litany, "Things are to be used, persons are to be loved." I must stop making other people look bad so that I look good, and quit making them feel bad so that I can feel better.

Are people that important? If the gospel is true, they are.

4

The Blessing of a Round-trip Ticket

A student describing her relationship with her parents said, "I'm an only child born late, so I guess I am pretty important to my mother and father. But I have to give them credit. When they send me a ticket to come home, it is always a round-trip ticket."

That is an important insight about family. To have a round-trip ticket means that you have freedom both to come and go. Some families only want you to go. Others only want you to come and never leave. The blessing is in having a family that gives you freedom to do both.

Of course, what that girl may not yet realize is that coming and going is a two-way street. Emotionally healthy parents are glad to have their children—and grandchildren—come, but also relieved to see them go.

Coming and going is but the external, physical manifestation of deeper and more significant agenda, which is the sorting out of the emotional and spiritual baggage we carry along with us on the trip. When that work can be done in an atmosphere warm with acceptance and respect, we are able to transfer from the older generation to the younger the best that has been accumulated. And we can do it without so burdening the next generation with our baggage that it can't accumulate some of its own.

The metaphor of the round-trip ticket suggests the universal need to go back home once you have left. Brilliant, lonely Thomas Wolfe, Asheville's gifted son, was not altogether correct when he wrote his now-famous title, *You Can't Go Home Again*. You not only can, you must. We all have to return to the place—spiritual, emotional, intellectual, and social—that gave us life. Not to do so is to be a rootless, displaced person.

Has it occurred to you that the prodigal son in Jesus' best-loved story did just that? He saw no alternative but to go home when "he came to himself." When he got his head screwed on straight, he realized that he needed to go home and set things right with his father. He would never be able to live like a man instead of a spoiled, self-indulgent boy, or a hog-herd until he made peace with his past.

It was not that the father was vindictive, demanding that the boy knuckle under and submit to parental authority as a price for being accepted at home. Nothing in Jesus' parable suggests that the father was an autocrat. He could not compel the boy to come home, even as he could not prevent his leaving. He wanted him to come home, but only when the younger son came to himself was he ready to go back.

But there are two sons in Jesus' story, and both had problems with their father. Son Number 1—the elder—was consumed with need for his father's approval, just as much as the younger—Number 2—was consumed with passion for wild self-indulgence. If the younger son was obsessed with leaving home to live with harlots, the elder was obsessed with circumspection lest he miss his father's approval. But he missed it anyway. He worked incessantly, driven by his starved ego to a life of joyless rectitude, but he never felt accepted, he never knew the warmth of fatherly affection. That he did not was certainly not the father's intention, and maybe not even his fault. But the reality was the same as perceived by this unblessed Number 1 son.

Thus we have one son who runs away because he does not value the father's blessing, only to discover later that it is necessary. And we have another son who is afraid to leave home at all because the father's blessing is the most important thing in his life, yet he never feels he has it. He is as much a stranger to the blessing of home as is the prodigal in the hog lot.

Even in disgrace there is hope for the younger son because he knows that he can go home. He had felt free to leave, and in the depths he feels free to return. It is true that he misunderstood what going home would entail. He supposed that his father would require an apology and impose the role of a hired man upon him. In that he was wrong, for the father had not lost a hired hand, he had lost a son.

But what is so sad about the elder son is that although he was a son he lived like a hired hand. He never felt free to leave or come back.

He spent his years working like a slave and resenting every minute of it, yet afraid to leave lest he cut himself off from the blessing he never experienced anyway.

What a sad conclusion to a life that had the bright promise of a loving relationship! Here is a man who has trapped himself into a no-win situation in which he can neither go nor come.